GRAPEVINE

*A Mother and Daughter's Tangled
Journey Through an Eating Disorder*

ALEXA DOERR &
MICHELLE DOERR

Grapevine: A Mother and Daughter's Tangled Journey Through an Eating Disorder
©Alexa Doerr & Michelle Doerr

Print ISBN: 979-8-35096-187-4
eBook ISBN: 979-8-35096-188-1

Note:

Because we have co-written this book and share our own unique perspectives, we have distinguished our voices by each using different font styles. Alexa's font style is what is shown in this sentence. *Michelle's font style is what is shown in this sentence.*

Disclaimer:

We have chosen to remove the names of schools, medical facilities, and counselors to protect privacy. Other than relatives, a family caregiver, and two close friends, we have changed or removed the names of all the other characters from our stories.

We are not licensed professionals. The ideas and suggestions found within this book should not be substituted for professional medical or mental health advice.

Content Warning:

This book contains topics that may be triggering to readers, including eating disorders, mental health concerns, suicide, divorce, and ableism related to autism spectrum disorder (also referred to as Asperger's or Asperger's Syndrome in this book, which was used at the time of diagnosis). Please read with care. We encourage you to seek support as needed.

For help:

Suicide and Crisis Lifeline: 988 [Spanish speaking services and for Deaf & Hard of Hearing]

ANAD (National Association of Anorexia Nervosa and Associated Disorders) Helpline: 1 (888) 375-7767 Monday-Friday, 9am-9pm CT

National Alliance for Eating Disorders Helpline: 1 (866) 662-1235 Monday-Friday, 9am-7pm ET

Check out the F.E.A.S.T website for eating disorder resources: https://www.feast-ed.org/

Dedication

To our beloved Cisco — a friend like no other

and the best supporter a family could have.

CONTENTS

Pruning

Changing Seasons

Harvest

Fruits of the Vine

Seeds Planted

INTRODUCTION

I sat in a room flooded with warm, natural light. There were delicate plants decorating the counter in the periphery of my gaze and piles of uplifting magazines to either side of me. Yet, somehow, it felt like the walls were caving in and an evil presence poisoned the air. Innocent and unaware, I was just 10-years-old sitting in the first waiting room of the many I would soon come to frequent. My parents and I sat in a row, the only ones in the room. I found some comfort in their presence but, though we were seemingly linked together in our stance, for some reason I felt we were all disconnected.

After some time had passed sitting in silence, a doctor came to escort us further into the facility. We were corralled into a smaller room with the same tan walls, but no windows, no pretty plants and much more serious pamphlets and pictures. There was definitely a tension in the air now. As the door shut and the space became confined, it felt as though we were all preparing to hear the most confidential secret the FBI had to offer.

But we weren't at the FBI. We were at a clinic for eating disorders.

Earlier, I had gone through all the tests that new doctors seem to find necessary: constricting my arm to check my blood pressure, insisting I undress so they could measure and manipulate every inch of my body and poking me with needles to test every fluid meant to be contained within me. It was not long ago I had the exact same tests done. Why doctors couldn't just send previous records to the next place was beyond me. It seemed everyone was out to torture me (I really hate needles, really really hate them). Though I felt the doctor sitting in the room with us was no exception, something was different. Instead of forceful and superior, they seemed wary of me.

All of the tests, questions, and judgment had previously been directed at me, but this conversation was avoidant.

"We think your daughter has an eating disorder."

No eye contact, no explanations, and no questions for me.

"It's not anorexia or bulimia, but it's not normal."

It was as if I was the opposite end of a magnet from this doctor, repelling their gaze, their discussion and their care. My mom was intensely focused. She was hooked on the doctor's every word like this was the newest gospel. My dad was quiet, somewhere between listening intently and lost in his own thoughts. I was just confused.

What kind of doctor "thinks" something is wrong? And then can't even give it a name? This didn't seem like a very competent doctor to me and, in fact, I didn't believe a word they said. I felt perfectly fine, looked perfectly fine and was perfectly fine brushing past these stupid accusations. I would need a lot more proof before I was going to believe there was anything I needed to worry about. Unfortunately for me, it didn't matter what I thought or felt. And even if it did, I lacked the introspection at that age to put into words what I was feeling.

Just looking over at the seriousness spread across my mom's face, I knew this was certainly not the last I'd be hearing about this mysterious, nameless disorder that was maybe there, maybe not. This was just the beginning. The beginning of my new reality.

I'm Alexa. Welcome to the story of my journey with an eating disorder. A little about me in 2024, when this book was published. I'm 24, a college graduate, a daughter to two supportive and loving parents, a sister to a very successful older brother, an animal lover and dog mom to my two pups whom I love deeply, a nature lover who loves to get out and camp, a goofball who loves to sing and doesn't mind letting loose and acting every now and then. Most of all, I'm a woman who just wants to support her fellow humans on their journey to happiness and fullness. I'm so grateful you are taking the time to glance into my life, even if it is focusing on one of the hardest parts of it. No matter what reason you've picked up this book, I hope you are able to take something from it because my whole purpose in writing it, really, is to let my experience be of service to others.

Before I fully dive in, I want to take a little time to explain what exactly this diagnosis looked like for me. Eating disorders look so different from person to person, so I want to paint a picture of what this meant for me, especially now that I understand it a little more.

Many people think of anorexia and bulimia when they think about eating disorders, but my eating disorder didn't fit the description for either of these diagnoses. The two main and visual concerns for my eating disorder were that I was not eating enough, and I ate very slowly. It would take me an hour or more to finish meals and, given the choice, my meal would be very small. I also had difficulties with textures of foods and a fear of choking. My preference was foods that were more liquid than solid in form (like ice cream, mashed potatoes, and applesauce), and those that weren't I would chew and swish around in my mouth until they were juice before I could swallow them. It seems so simple to say it now but, wow, did these struggles rule my life for quite some time.

And this didn't just affect my life, it affected people around me as well. Which leads me to something else you should know about this book. Because I believe multiple perspectives can help illuminate an experience, I've enlisted someone else to help me with this book.

Hi, I'm Michelle, Alexa's mom. I'm in my mid-fifties and I wasn't always interested in being a mom. Plans change. Before Alexa's eating disorder entered our lives, we were a typically functioning family that experienced both joys and challenges. Our days were filled with shared moments of play with family and friends, engaging in games, outdoor activities, and enjoying family camping trips. Additionally, we found solace and community through fellowship at our church. Parenting presented its own set of difficulties, particularly as we navigated Nicolas's (referred to as Nick in the rest of the book) speech challenges that surfaced at 18 months and eventually led to an Autism Spectrum Disorder diagnosis by the age of 3. Despite these early challenges, our family thrived on love and togetherness.

Through the challenges of parenting, I have come to realize that motherhood has taught me more about who I am than any other thing I've done.

In fact, I wouldn't have my own company doing personal and leadership development work if I hadn't experienced raising my two amazing children.

Through the counseling we received, I came to understand and embrace the psychology of Alfred Adler. I use those principles in much of my work in the conservation community. I am a huge nature lover and say I like to connect people to themselves, to others and to the Earth. I also love camping. I have a seasonal RV site that I consider my sanctuary, which I now share with my loving partner.

We don't have a perfect life, but we do have many moments of perfection. This book and some of the conversations around it have contributed to those moments of perfection. I am proud of both of my children, especially when embracing their overcoming stories.

Together, we are going to share our perspectives of what it was like going through the journey of battling and recovering from an eating disorder. Some parts will be written by me and some will be written by my mom, and we'll both share some thoughts about what the other person has said. You'll come to find that there are some moments in our stories that align, but there are also others that seem to contradict each other. While neither perspective may hold the entire truth, they do hold our individual truths. And we're ok with leaving it at that. It's a demonstration of human experience in its most raw and real forms.

We would also like to note that many other perspectives are not included in this book. Two main missing perspectives are those of my dad and my brother, Nick, who each played a huge part in our eating disorder journey and continue to be such valued parts of our lives. Other perspectives unrepresented include those of relatives, friends and our care team. Although these perspectives are not included to their fullest in this book, we want to acknowledge their existence and value.

I would also like to emphasize that I am writing my perspective from what I remember of my ten-year-old thoughts and feelings. I wanted to share honestly what my mindset was like at that time in hopes that it will help another young person better put into words what they are experiencing or help a parent gain perspective on what their child may be similarly going through when struggling with mental illness. I have since gained additional knowledge, awareness and skills that I also try to share a bit of towards the end of this book.

I occasionally journaled during that time but did not track every detail. So, some of my recollections are based on the journal and some are not. I've also done my best to recall these situations without embellishment.

As you read, we hope you'll be as nonjudgmental as we were required to be with each other. These were difficult stories to tell. They are the truths we felt at that time. We acknowledged that with each other and we desire the same from our readers. Try to sit with us when you can and imagine how difficult this must have been.

Our book unfolds in six distinct sections, each capturing a crucial phase in our journey.

First, Seeds Planted is an introduction to our story and the roots of our experiences. Taking Root contains the initial two months around the diagnosis of the eating disorder. Tangled Vines is approximately three months of navigating the complexities and challenges of addressing the eating disorder head-on. Pruning unfolds over a year, chronicling the process of improvement and recovery. Changing Seasons spans six years, focusing on the ongoing efforts of weight maintenance and the development of new ways of being. Harvest is our lessons learned from the entirety of our experience. Finally, Fruits of the Vine is a snapshot of our current state as this book is published, offering a glimpse into the outcomes and growth that have taken root over time.

With that, welcome to our eating disorder journey.

Taking Root

THE CALL

I had just come up from my home office to take a break and stretch my legs in the kitchen when the home phone rang. It was the nurse from the grade school. I knew that usually isn't a good sign, so I remember that I sat on the end chair on our island, gut churning, heart racing, and braced myself for what I was about to hear.

That day, February 26, 2010, is when I received "the call." That moment changed how I relate to my little girl forever. This call was immediately stressful because first and foremost, there had been a fairly recent school kidnapping in the area (the girl was found safe). I knew something wasn't quite right with Alexa, but I couldn't put my finger on it. I knew it wasn't just a simple illness because the kids had left for school that day doing well.

The nurse proceeded to tell me someone (I don't recall who) had overheard three girls at lunch making a pact not to eat and Alexa was among them. I remember the news hitting me in the gut and thinking "What? That sounds crazy!" The conversation verified what I'd already been feeling, however — that there was something wrong. I knew her slow eating and swishing food through her teeth could be related to what the nurse heard. I was not expecting this weird pact thing, though, and I didn't know what to think about it.

I already recognized at meals that she would take much longer than everyone else. I excused it because I eat way too fast myself. I often wished I took more time so I would savor meals as well as probably eat less.

More alarming, however, was Alexa's frustration with her dog, Cisco. When they were in their dog agility training, she was noticeably short on patience with her dog, which she loves more than anything. She just wasn't herself.

I suppose I could have been avoiding digging into what Alexa was facing because we were already in the midst of health issues with Nick, my son, who was 11 and a year older than Alexa. So, there was probably a moment of "Oh shit, not something else!"

Nick had some stomach issues, a low iron level and a few allergies that we'd been dealing with for several months already. The doctors could not quite get to the heart of the problem. Plus, he had Asperger's Syndrome, diagnosed around age 5. Parenting had been more challenging than normal for most of the time I'd been doing it.

Between my job, raising a son on the autism spectrum and now this, I felt numb. I didn't have any strong emotions, perhaps because I was already overwhelmed. While I had clues about what might be happening with Alexa, I didn't have a definitive answer about anything. All I could do was muster up the energy to take the next step, which was to call the doctor.

I'd already been seeing my doctor for about twenty years. She knew everything about me and my family and I trusted her most for advice on what to do with Alexa. Alexa didn't really have a regular doctor because, except for regular check-ups, she rarely had to go. She had low hemoglobin levels a few years prior which eventually sent us to a university clinic. The experts there said she'd likely grow out of it. Other than that, she was mostly a healthy, vibrant child.

I know how much she hated the doctor's office after that early diagnosis, so I didn't tell her about making the appointment until the week we had to go. There was some crying and even though I don't recall specific words, I know she was attempting to talk me out of it. She also knew that once I've made a decision like this, there isn't much she can do but follow along.

While we drove, there was pretty much silence (perhaps alongside a few sniffles). I'm not one to talk much during such a sober time, either. What was there to say? I think the numbing I felt since the call prevented me from thinking more clearly about what she might need.

When we arrived at the doctor's office, she did a regular exam — ears, nose, throat, temperature, weight, height etc. Other than her weight, she seemed in good health but the weight dip was pretty substantial.

Alexa had gone from 50th percentile to below what the growth charts record. That was a significant enough drop to be considered serious. I told her what the school nurse had told me about the pact with the other girls. She asked Alexa some minor questions, but mostly directed her attention to me and what I'd need to do.

My doctor eventually recommended a clinic in the Twin Cities metropolitan area about an hour from our house. She said it was specifically for eating disorders, which she believed might be happening. The facility was well respected. I was able to book an appointment within two weeks for blood work and a physical.

In between the first call and our appointment, we didn't talk much about it. What was there to talk about? We didn't have any official diagnosis. It was a scary time for me not knowing what I was dealing with. Would she need to go to an in-patient facility? I felt like I lacked support inside my family and there wasn't really anyone to talk to. So, I just dug into my work until we had to face our first appointment.

Sitting at the doctor's office for a single appointment is not fun, much less for a whole day with a child who would rather get her teeth pulled and absolutely feared the blood work. Plus, who wants to hear, officially, the terrible news that your daughter is trying to kill herself in the slowest way possible? Perhaps that seems dramatic, but that's what it felt like. I kept thinking — how could this have happened? How did I not see it earlier? Why would someone choose that as a way to live? And, of course, the internal judgment about being a "good" mom.

One month to the day from "the call," we had all day appointments with her assigned case worker, doctor, nutritionist, and counselor. During that month, my emotions ran the gauntlet, but I think the biggest ones were shame and guilt. How could I not have noticed sooner?

During that time in our lives, the kids' school district was dissolving rather than consolidating, which was a first for the state of Minnesota. That meant our kids would have to switch schools. The initial appointments came in the middle of Alexa's first year at the new school.

Alexa was in fourth grade, so she was at the elementary school; Nick was in fifth grade at the middle school. That meant that they didn't even have each other to rely on at breaks or recess for the first time in their lives. Looking back, I think the health issues they both experienced during that time were related to changing schools. I didn't take the time to sit down with them and process how they were feeling. There wasn't a decision to be made or discussed. This was happening for everyone in the area.

Fear was the other big emotion. When I learned about Nick's Asperger's Syndrome, I felt relief — something to explain some of the behaviors he demonstrated. That was not a death sentence. It was the name of something we could work with. I'm not saying it wasn't hard or painful, but I didn't have the same fear of death that seemed to come with the diagnosis of an eating disorder.

The future was so uncertain for all of us at that time. I wasn't sure if Nick would be okay with so much chaos going on, along with the added impact of losing the paraprofessional with whom he'd spent most of his educational life. This was different. I think there was a sense of grief here. My bright-eyed, positive, and creative daughter was slowly disappearing, mentally, emotionally and physically. The thought of losing her was terrifying.

My way of dealing with it is just to shut all those emotions down (or at least not show them in public) and "get to work" on solving the problem.

"Get to work" for me meant diving into my job but also starting my research on dealing with eating disorders, much like I'd done with Asperger's. We were in a time of survival — far from a thriving family. Information was my way of surviving.

Interestingly enough, in my information gathering period, I didn't gather more facts from the nurse, teachers or anyone else at school. I think it was easy for me to believe this was a pact, because then I didn't have to point as much blame at myself.

Thankfully, we had caught this early enough that in-patient care was not required. This started us on a process that would take months of weekly travel to the Twin Cities.

* * * * * *

As I am writing this, I still feel that guilt. I should and could have done better to prevent and navigate this. My self-compassion comes from knowing that I didn't have better parenting skills because I didn't see them as a child either. Sharing these stories is a way for me to further process the guilt and practice self-compassion. In sharing, I hope to help others process and sit with what is happening sooner than later.

Eating disorders are hard; perhaps one of the hardest things one can face. The journey could be long. I hope in some way, we give ideas to help others through the journey so they don't have to face it alone.

Alexa's Perspective:

Mom didn't tell me about the nurse's call. It wasn't until much later that I learned about the school nurse claiming a group of girls, me included, had made a pact to stop eating. I was baffled at the notion, just as confused as my mom was. I had just met these girls when I started at my new school. We were friendly, but hardly knew each other well enough to be real, close-knit friends.

I have always been a pretty logical person. How would it even work to "stop eating?" Would we just stop eating at school, or at home too? How would anyone know what I did at home? What would we even be doing this for? Why would I be talking about food with people I practically just met? All of those questions went through my head as mom relayed the news to me then. These questions still stump me to this day.

Since I had no knowledge of "the call" in the beginning and was not told why I was being taken to the doctor, I felt a lot of confusion and lack of control. This was paired with frustration about going to the doctor's office which was already a traumatic and unpleasant experience for me from earlier events in my life.

HARD TO SWALLOW

It seemed as if we bounced from "diagnosis" to full treatment team and plan in place in the blink of an eye. My mom's calendar was suddenly filled with appointment after appointment. I went from a sweet, innocent girl to nothing more than a diseased patient. I felt like my identity was thrown away like the bathroom trash.

I was referred to a facility specializing in eating disorder treatment. When we pulled into the parking lot, we were greeted with rows upon rows of spaces to choose from. The place was huge. Obviously, this was somewhere important if enough people would come to fill the parking spaces provided. But why were we here? I didn't think anything was wrong with me, but the expansiveness of the lot and building sent a frightened chill down my spine.

To the left of the entrance was a long strip of gardens with an overhang along the entire stretch of sidewalk leading to the front door. It reminded me of bus stops, where there's two pillars supporting an overhead roof so people can wait outside and not get wet in the rain, except there were many pillars that seemed to go on and on. I didn't understand why such a structure was necessary. It made the walk from the car to inside feel like a march to prison. The building itself was burnt orange, an ugly color I thought, but it had large adjoining windows to let in natural light, probably to fake a sense of brightness and happiness that didn't actually exist there.

There was a lot to notice as we stepped through the front door. To our left was a large seating area with different colored chairs and some geometrical decorations hanging from the ceiling. What caught my attention most was the large, black piano where a man sat calmly, tinkering at the shiny keys. The song reverberated throughout the lobby area; it was calm and soft but filled the space. I couldn't help but feel a little comfort listening to his song and watching him play like nothing else existed. I pointed him out to my mom, hoping she would think I was being positive, like maybe if I acted happy about being at this place it could all end. She stopped and smiled, but then kept moving further into the building.

Straight ahead, there was a tall reception desk with a woman glancing up from her computer, waiting for me and my mom to reach her so she could greet us. Behind the counter just to the right was a wide hallway leading to a room with tall tables and chairs and walls filled with floor to ceiling windows. I would later discover this was the cafeteria. To the right of the entrance was a block-like, winding staircase that led to the mysterious floors above.

My mom did all of the talking and answered the check-in questions when we made it to the front desk. My mind was racing. I didn't know what was going to happen and this was all so foreign to me. After collecting the necessary paperwork, the receptionist motioned to the staircase and gave us directions.

Second floor.

Take a right.

At the end of that hallway take a left.

Go past the first reception desk.

Stop and check in at the second reception desk.

I absorbed every word, hoping that if I focused on that instead I would forget everything else. I led the way up the stairs to a large door labeled "2." The staircase was dark and cold and I was starting to get more nervous as we made it closer to our destination. The hallways leading to the final reception desk were divided by offices and nooks with large windows, a couple chairs, and side tables with magazines.

Mom checked us in at the second reception desk and we were asked to take a seat and wait for someone to call us back. We shuffled over to the nearest nook, where I took a peek out the window. This window overlooked a walking path that had a grove of trees on the other side and flowers planted here and there along the way. The sky was blue with fluffy white clouds. It was as picturesque as it gets. Out there, the world seemed normal. But I was stuck in here, only wishing I could be out there.

"Alexa?" I turned around to see a smiling young nurse. She introduced herself then escorted me down the hallway with my mom closely following. We turned the corner and the nurse stopped at the first room on the left, which was a stereotypical doctor's examination room. A blue spotted gown was folded neatly on the examination table. "Step right in here and put the gown on. You can crack the door when you are ready," she said with a smile as she slowly closed the door behind us. I didn't hear any footsteps walking away, so I whispered to my mom "do I have to take my underwear off?" She told me I could leave on my socks and underwear, so I quickly threw the rest of my clothes onto one of the chairs along the wall, cracked the door, and sat on the exam table.

"Wow, that was speedy!" The nurse set her materials down in front of the computer at the nurse's desk and then stepped by the door. "First, we'll get your height and weight."

The measuring rod and weight scale were between the nurse's desk and the door. I stood still and straight while the nurse planted the level on my head to record my height, then stepped onto the square metal scale on the floor. The nurse went to the computer and turned it away from me.

At first, I was confused that there wasn't an electronic panel for the numbers to display my weight. It didn't take me long to realize that the weight reading was on the computer, and I was not allowed to look at it. Why was it that these people, whom I had never met before, didn't trust me? I honestly had no idea what they thought I was going to do with that number, but I was upset that they immediately put me in a box. The "untrustworthy girl with a problem" box.

The nurse asked a few routine questions before letting us know that the doctor would be in soon. I sat and stared around the room, avoiding eye contact with my mom while nervously fidgeting my leg back and forth. Several minutes later the doctor entered the room. She was short and stout, had dark hair, and was probably in her fifties. She didn't have the same demeanor as the younger nurse; she didn't smile and her voice wasn't cheery. She was very to the point and jumped right into her examination.

The doctor did her own set of tests, taking my blood pressure, measuring my heart rate, pressing on my abdomen asking for any signs of pain, and then she asked me a bunch of questions.

"Do you smoke?"

"Do you drink alcohol?"

"Are you sexually active?"

I was astonished that she was asking these questions to a 10-year-old, and so nonchalantly. Of course, the answer to all of these things was "no." If she knew anything about me, she'd know I was top of my class, a little oblivious when it came to substance use, and by no means a daredevil — all qualities that would never allow me to do such things.

Right away I knew I did not like her. She felt heartless, assuming, and unkind. Next, she pulled a paper from my file and handed it to me. The paper had nine drawn women figures in swimsuits with numbers running one through nine above them, a number for each woman. The woman labeled "1" had small features: boney arms and legs and a tight waist. Gradually the women from 2-8 gained larger features, leading to the woman labeled "9" who had rounded arms and legs and a protruding waist.

"Which one do you think you look like?" She handed me a pencil to circle the drawn figure of my choice. I hesitated and looked from the doctor back to the pictures confused and a little annoyed. Couldn't she use her eyes just as well as I could? She shouldn't need me to circle an image to know what my figure looks like; she could look right at the real me — she was right now.

I scanned the drawings and couldn't decide between the woman labeled "2" and the woman labeled "3." None of these pictures really looked like me: I didn't have a "womanly" figure, I was just a kid, so of course I was a little smaller than lots of other people. I'd always been a little smaller than the rest of my class, but I also didn't feel like I was tiny enough to have bones protruding. I decided to go with "2," thinking that's what the doctor would likely say I was, then thrust the paper and pencil back to the doctor.

"Just wait," she motioned the paper back toward my lap. "Now circle which one you want to look like." I was honestly fine with how I looked. I had never really thought of my visual appearance as being a choice I could make. However, people were obviously having problems with me being relatively small, so I decided to jump a few steps up to "4" to hopefully get them off my back. Maybe if they saw I wanted the changes that they so clearly did, they would see nothing was mentally wrong with me and say case closed.

She finished her interrogation and tests, shared a few words with my mom, and soon it was time to be passed on to the next set of tests. I was told to put my clothes back on, and then my mom and I could head back to the window nook where we had waited before. I tried flipping through magazines, but my eyes just glossed over the pages, I couldn't focus on the pictures and words over the nerves of being in this place. The next woman that walked into the waiting room, smiling, asked for me to follow her. "I'll bring her back here in a bit, we'll be just down the hall," she said to my mom, who seemed undisturbed by this stranger whisking me away.

As we walked down the hallway out of sight of my mom, the mood of smiley, calming provider quickly disappeared. We entered another room that had only a table and chair, with no windows, which made the mood even more tense. I had no idea what I was doing with this woman, but I didn't like the vibe in the room. I just knew something bad was about to happen.

The provider wasted no time and cut right to the chase, handing me an apple slice. "I just want you to eat this for me." She stared me down with her arms folded across her clipboard. Why would she drag me all this way just to give me an apple to eat? I wasn't even hungry. I was so confused, I almost wanted to ask her to explain, but decided against it (I've always been a little shy with new people) and slowly drew the apple slice to my mouth and took a bite. She didn't speak for a few seconds, and I was starting to feel a little calmer, when she did what I could never have expected.

"Ok, now swallow."

I was flabbergasted. "What?"

"Swallow." She gestured her hand toward me, as if that would speed the process. I slowed my chewing from the shock and avoided her aggressive stare.

"Swallow now!"

Even if I had been ready to swallow at that moment, I suddenly felt as though my throat was cemented shut. The more she told me to swallow, the less likely it was going to happen. It was as if the word itself was preventing me from doing so. If I were to swallow this bite now, I would surely choke. Her watchful eyes punched my gut and I felt as though this was never going to end. My mind was suddenly racing, plotting ways to escape. But she was standing in front of the only way out.

I waited for a pause in between her demands to swallow, and quickly gulped down the piece of apple before she could say the word again. It felt as if a rock was forcing its way down my throat. I could feel it slowly make its way down towards my stomach, and I was so uncomfortable. My heart was beating fast as I wondered if, at any second, the apple would stop its movement and choke me to death.

"Take another bite."

I felt like I was being tortured. What did this lady want from me? Feeling hopeless, I took another small bite of the apple slice. Only a few seconds later the demands came again.

"Swallow, swallow now."

It didn't take me quite as long to meet the demand since I took a smaller bite, but I still had to force it down my throat. My muscles were tight, I was sweating, everything about the situation was making me feel constricted. I closed my eyes and waited, hoping this could be over.

"Alright, you can take the rest of that with you. I'll walk you back to your mom," she said as she jotted some final notes on her clipboard.

I couldn't get out of that room fast enough. I kept my distance from the woman, walking ahead a lot faster than she was. I didn't say anything to my mom when I got back, just quickly sat across from her and stared out the window. I was violated, and hurt, and scared, and at that moment I didn't feel safe with anyone.

When we got up to leave, I waited for my mom to lead the way and lagged behind. I clenched the last bite of apple in my hand where it was out of sight. I couldn't stand the thought of eating it, not after all that, so when no one was looking, I threw the last bite of apple into the garbage. It was only the first day at this treatment center, but right then I knew that I hated it. And that I would be perfectly happy never eating an apple again.

Mom's Perspective:

What I remember on that first day is feeling a pang in my gut as we walked inside. I was so overwhelmed with what we were about to face. I didn't yet know if this was severe enough to require in-patient services and that scared the shit out of me. I already knew Alexa did not want to be there. Any suggestion of residential care would have sent her into a tailspin and me into a state of complete overwhelm, shock, grief, guilt, and shame. I did not notice much about the outside of the building at all — I didn't care. I just want to get in and get out.

I recall the first check-in, but different from Alexa. I remember going to a room on the right side where we met our case worker. I am thinking that Alexa stayed out in a small waiting room while I talked to the case worker in another. She gave me the heads up that we'd be meeting with a team of people, doctors, nutritionists, counselors and perhaps some others as well. We went over insurance information, and I felt marginally grateful that this would be covered to some extent. At least I wasn't going to have to worry about depleting savings, although I wasn't yet sure how much and how long this would take. I remember this area being white, with no windows. Very sterile. It was from here when we had to go up the stairs and over to the doctor's office.

Alexa did lead the way, which kind of surprised me. I assumed I'd have to drag her from place to place. When we got down the final hallway, there was an option to pick some chairs right out in the hallway or the little nook that Alexa described. She chose the nook which had a nice view of the woods behind the facility. I was grateful for the light and something to look at besides magazines.

In the doctor's office, Alexa sat on the table while I sat on a chair next to the doctor's computer. She ran through a series of tests and questions directed mostly at Alexa. I, too, hate that they can't just use records, especially when it comes to taking blood of any kind. Alexa had a blood issue when she was much younger and they had to poke her so many times, she now has an extreme fear of needles. I was hoping we would not have to do blood work that day as that would have added an extra layer of tension to an already overwhelming experience. Luckily, we did not. I know even though they have access to our regular doctors' records, there is always a baseline required when checking into a new facility. I know this is part of the process, so I just went along with the flow.

As the doctor handed Alexa the body image chart, I was nervous about how she would respond. I didn't think she had any body image issues and I assume that was what this was for, but at this point, I didn't know what to think. My gut was tight and I prayed silently that she'd pick an image that made sense. I was relieved and grateful when she didn't choose the larger images — I think she chose a reasonable image of what she was. My assumption was that if she chose a body grossly larger than she was that we'd have some additional concerns. That was not the case, and the topic did not come up again.

The doctor told me that they do not allow the child (or client, I assume) to see the scale as standard procedure. I guessed some, when seeing the number, might get even more aggressive in their pursuit of "small." This was the beginning of the trickery involved in this disorder.

I was always a little uneasy when they took her away without me. As a mom, I feel like I had to side with the professionals, at least until they proved *otherwise. I did not, at all, like the fact that she was being taken away with a person I had just met. What choice did I have? I also didn't know what they were doing or saying. I also wasn't confident I'd know what Alexa was saying or doing. She was generally a joyous and mannerly child, but she was not happy with me. I didn't know if she was angry enough to seek some kind of retaliation. When you think about what you see on TV, you never know when someone is going to randomly take your kids away unjustifiably. When she returned from her brief visit, she did not say a word.*

From that first examination, we were dismissed. I didn't ask about the swallowing issue as I assumed it would be discussed in future meetings. I stopped at the appointment desk and made appointments for our next visit, which would include the doctor again, a nutritionist and Alexa's counselor. I carried my calendar along with me so I could make appointments right there. Because we drove over an hour to get there and we'd be visiting multiple times per week, I asked if it would be possible to get all those appointments near each other. Every time we visited required 2.5 hours or so in drive time and up to 3 hours in visits. I had to begin navigating my time around them, my full-time job while also caring for Nick, his issues and our home.

Insanity time, if it hadn't already hit, was about to begin.

BEHIND THE CAMERA

Unfortunately for me, that first day of appointments was just the start of my experiences being watched or feeling violated while eating. The woman who had done the swallowing assessment (I guess that's what all that torture was supposed to accomplish) had requested that my mom video tape me eating at home. At the time, I figured my mom would kindly nod at the suggestion and then not follow through with such a weird request. I was wrong.

I had received a small, brown recording camera as a gift from my grandparents to video the training I was doing with my dog, Cisco. I was so excited about that gift. I spent a lot of time making sure it was set up just right for each shoot — set to record and not photo and learning how to download the videos once I had taken them. I had gotten quite a bit of joy from using something that was mine, to do something that I loved, to show everyone else what I was passionate about.

When my mom pulled the tripod with my video camera out at dinner one night and set it about a foot away from me on the table, I was furious.

"Why are you using my camera?"

"We have to record you eating, and this is the only camera I could find. Don't worry, I won't delete anything already on here and I'll be sure to take my videos off myself." Her voice sounded matter of fact and kindly explanatory. No big deal. I was going to continue arguing, but I could feel the slightest twinge of guilt in her demeanor, so I decided to let that issue go.

My family had already finished eating and my dad and brother had gone about their lives, so it was just me, my half-eaten plate of food, my mom, and my video camera. I looked down at my food and slowly started stirring pieces around, avoiding the inevitable.

"Well, you better get to eating." My mom stood behind the camera, keeping her eyes on me while also drifting her eyes impatiently away every now and then. I could tell we were both uncomfortable with the situation, so I wasn't sure why we were even doing this.

In my head, there were two choices. One, I could start eating and be incredibly uncomfortable for minutes on end. Or I could just not eat and keep waiting for mom to crack and give up on the idea of videoing me. The latter seemed the most reasonable option; I knew I could put up a good fight. I also knew the part of mom that was uncomfortable and guilty couldn't hold on forever. I could.

I kept still and swirled the food around my plate, averting my eyes from the camera at all costs. I felt like a lab rat, bright lights shining on me, a camera set up to view my every move and all that would matter was the "mad scientist" analyzing the film afterwards for any evidence of who knows what.

It didn't matter how the rat felt. I was stuck as someone else's experiment.

I didn't even know who would be watching my video or what they would be doing with it, but I felt like I could picture it. Some brunette lady in her early 30s perched over a computer, jotting notes on a clipboard of every little oddity she could see in the video. I imagined her noticing how I only ate 5 peas at a time instead of 7, how I chew on the right side and then switch to the left, how I eat with a fork instead of a spoon. I imagined her taking note of how my hair is too short, my body is too thin, and my presence is too awkward. I imagined her judging our house in the background and my conversation if I spoke. Judgment, judgment, judgment, all from a short video clip of me eating, instead of taking the time to know anything about me.

"Alexa, just eat so we can move on."

My mom kept urging me, but I was not about to give up so easily. I took one pea and pulled it to my front teeth, biting it in half and tossing it in my mouth, just to show I "ate something." Of course, this didn't satisfy my mom. I knew it wouldn't, but I couldn't stand to eat when I could feel the judgment behind the camera. My throat felt tight again like it had during the swallowing assessment, I could practically hear "swallow, swallow now!" ringing in my ears.

"I don't want to eat in front of a camera."

I didn't have the energy or the knowledge to explain in words why I didn't want this, except to say that I didn't want it. I could tell my mom thought I was just trying to use excuses, but her patience was also running low.

"Just eat a few bites and then we can be done with the camera." I still had the urge to fight on but gave in to take one normal size bite. I sat looking straight forward, avoiding the camera slightly to my right. My bites were slow and hesitant; I was barely making any progress on actually chewing the food. It was more like I was moving the food slowly around my mouth. I couldn't ignore the pressure of the camera pushing against me. I wanted to cry, but my face stayed expressionless and cold. Many minutes went by and I managed to finish maybe two bites of food, but we had both had enough.

"Fine, that video will have to be good enough." My mom stopped the recording and set the camera on a side counter. "You need to keep eating though." I looked down at my food, disheartened. I didn't feel the same weight on me that the camera had given, but now I felt defeated. I wasn't hungry and couldn't shake away the feeling of being judged. The food on my plate seemed like my enemy. Whenever I was in the presence of food, it seemed there was always something I was doing wrong and it made the food feel wrong.

Over the course of the next twenty minutes or so, I finished about half of my food. I continually stared at the plate, sadness looming over me. But my mom and I were both done trying to fight this battle.

"Can I just be done?" I didn't look up at her when the quiet words came out of my mouth. She gave a look to me and to the plate, then let out a big sigh. A look crossed her face that was kind of an eye roll, but more of loss than of annoyance.

"Fine, that's good enough for tonight." She picked up my plate to empty its contents into the trash and put the plate in the dishwasher. I could tell she was feeling defeated, but I don't think she realized that I was feeling it too. Earlier I would've considered this a victory; I managed to overpower mom, so I didn't have to finish my food. But instead of feeling victorious, all I felt was crushed. Moments like this were starting to consume my life; three meals a day plus snacks, food constantly breathing down my neck. Just like that dark room from the eating disorder center, I didn't see any logical escape. We didn't speak for the rest of the night and I went to bed utterly dejected.

Mom's Perspective:

To get a picture of what eating was like at home, the counselor asked if I'd be able to videotape Alexa eating at home. I said I might be able to do it but wasn't sure. She said it would be helpful in treating her and to do my best.

That same night, I thought I would give it a try. We had simple foods to eat. I recall mashed potatoes, peas and some kind of meat. The meat was always the hardest. Peas and potatoes could easily be sloshed between her teeth, back and forth, forever, before she swallowed each bite. It was painful to watch, much less having to videotape the whole thing.

My parents had gotten her a cute little video camera for Christmas so she could record her dog training (and whatever else she wanted). I had a larger video camera, but I really didn't want that thing to be in her face. I thought maybe the small camera would seem less invasive. I made sure I used a new tape, so I didn't accidentally erase something she had recorded.

She sat in the middle chair at the table and I sat to her left, holding the video camera against the table at an angle, so I didn't have to hold it up the whole time. I knew this was going to take a while. I hated taking the video because it felt like an invasion of privacy for all of us. I thought to myself "Who acts the same knowing they're on video as they would in private when eating?" This was early in the process, and I had no choice but to follow the requests of the professionals so we could set a plan for navigating this disorder. I was required to get past my discomfort for the betterment of my child. I had to do whatever it took; if a video was required, I had to do it.

I tried to talk about other things but that felt weird too, to know they'd be hearing our conversations. I decided to just sit there and get it done. But I could see she was struggling. Trying to hide her face from the camera as much as she could. I was feeling kind of sad for her, and for me, having to do this stupid assignment.

I think at some point about halfway in, when the rest of us were finished, Nick expressed some words of encouragement, telling Alexa just to work to get it done so we could all be done with it. He wasn't comfortable with this either. I appreciated the attempt because if anyone could reach her it was Nick. He left the table and then it was just me and Alexa, as it was most of the time.

Alexa fought it for a while and then eventually, with those sad and defeated eyes, looked at me and asked if we could be done. We'd both had enough. I thought to myself that if I didn't capture what they needed, then we were going to have to find another way. I felt ashamed, in a way. This didn't seem right and I was a part of it. When I told Alexa it was enough, I cleaned up the plates and went off on my own for a short bike ride. There was just enough light for me to get one in, and I needed the time to myself to take some pent-up energy out on my bike. I felt sad, defeated, disgusted and ashamed but I couldn't let her see it — I had to be the strong one.

THE MEALTIME MAZE

Meals were an incredible chore. During the first six months, I spent 6-8 hours on food — planning it, packing it, prepping it, eating it, and then waiting and watching Alexa finish hers.

During our first appointment with the nutritionist, I was given basic information about nutrition — what makes a serving, how many servings of each food group was needed in a day, as well as a list of examples to show how many servings each food offered. There was also a list of fast-food restaurants and the servings in some of their common meals. The servings Alexa had to have each day to gain weight was listed in a table.

Requirements	Monday	Tuesday	Wednesday	Thursday	Friday	Saturday	Sunday
Breakfast							
½ protein							
Milk							
Grain							
Fat							
AM snack							
Fruit							
Grain							
Lunch							
½ protein							
Milk							
Fruit							
Vegetable							
Grain							
Fat							
PM Snack							
Grain							
Dinner							
1 protein							
Milk							
Fruit							
Vegetable							
Grain							
Fat							
Bedtime Snack							
Fat							
Dessert							

This was incredibly overwhelming. While I had the basic information and a "meal plan" per se, I still had to put the real plan together from food we were used to. Sample menus weren't provided other than the fast food stuff and I didn't want that to be where we got the majority of our food.

To make this effort more efficient, as well as reduce the anxiety I felt thinking about food and the eating disorder, I turned to weekly planning. It's also true that I do not like to cook. I can and I'm not bad at it, I just don't enjoy it. The more time I could get away from thinking about food, the better.

I accomplished my planning in several ways. First, I made lists of favorite and familiar foods that would meet the requirements for each meal, along with favorite snacks. I also made lists of the fruits and vegetables that each child liked and disliked. Most of the time, I would try to choose fruits and veggies they both liked, but to maintain variety, sometimes I provided each of them with their own favorites.

I created a weekly spreadsheet that included the requirements for each meal for each day of the week, according to the table. I used this weekly planning tool for over a year and saved all of them because I could easily repeat instead of starting anew. Most of the time I used Sunday evening to plan out the week. It usually took me a couple of hours, by the time I reviewed my meal list and considered how the week's events might affect the time we had to cook and eat. Planning also helped me make my grocery list so I only had to shop once a week. Anywhere I could gain some time, I used it. The weekly plan also worked well to post and share with others who might be helping with meals. If Robert knew what had to be made, I could leave the recipe out and he could do some of the prepping so I could keep working or, on occasion, get outside for some exercise.

Meal prepping, at times, created some "pre-anxiety" for me, so any time I could get some help saved me some struggle during meals. Just thinking about what was ahead for the week and the long list of to-dos felt exasperating at times.

This plan was particularly important when I traveled for work. I would post the plan on the fridge or lay it out on the counter so the kids could see what was up next. This was helpful for Nick who liked to know things ahead of time. I wished I had thought of it sooner.

Along with the meal plan came serving sizes. Following the nutritionist's instructions, we plated everything. Alexa wouldn't have any choices for a while.

When school was in session, I also printed out the school lunch menu for the month. Thankfully, they prepared it a month at a time instead of weekly — more time saved, if even a few minutes each week. Every little bit helped.

When I printed it out, I would hand it to each of the kids and they would use a star to indicate which meals they liked and an X for those they didn't. The meals they liked I would write into the plan. On days they didn't like the school meals, I had to plan the packed lunches.

Truthfully, I wish I had paid more attention to the school lunches earlier. There were probably many days when they didn't eat much at school. Although, I do cut myself some slack here. We didn't have choices about what we ate at school when I was growing up.

Some Sundays I also spent time looking for recipes to add to my meal list. Often, I searched for recipes that were already high in calories or that could be adjusted to increase the calories. One recipe I remember was Overnight French Toast, where I used full fat whipping cream and the densest bread I thought the kids would eat. Now, this was an extra struggle for me. I come from a family that is on the round side. While I wasn't huge, I did not need the extra calories myself. So, every time I had to make food with fuller fat or higher calories, I suppose I also felt a little resentment.

I don't recall talking about my size or weight, but I sometimes wonder if I did more than I thought. My struggle with weight started early. To this day, I still remember a horse accident that landed me in the hospital with a concussion and cracked skull in seventh grade. I lost 20 pounds. I was glad that happened, or I can't imagine what size I would be today. I suspect some of my food frustration was also due to my lack of self-control around food — I see it, I eat it. So, making food such a large part of my life wasn't helping me much.

Because I didn't like to cook, I had many go-to meals that allowed me to only cook twice a week and use leftovers for the rest. As a Minnesotan, I had many hotdishes on the list. Pasta dishes like lasagna and chicken alfredo were common too. Thankfully, we lived on a farm and had plenty of access to meat. We ate a lot of roasts, ham, pork chops and hamburgers. We did have to buy poultry and made chicken nuggets, drumsticks and roasted turkey frequently.

We went through a lot of peanut butter. PBJ (peanut butter & jelly) sandwiches, on toast, on bananas, on crackers — peanut butter was one of my best friends. We also had plenty of quick foods like hot dogs, pizza, grilled cheese and store-bought chicken nuggets.

I liked doing egg salad or fried egg sandwiches because it met so many of the requirements for protein, grains and fat plus had a good number of calories. It was also easy to make and the rest of the family really liked them (although the rest of them would prefer egg salad without celery).

Ice cream was the other lifesaver. Most bedtime snacks included either a bowl of it, an ice cream sandwich, or a root beer float. We also made many trips to the local Dairy Queen or the small drive-in restaurant for our favorite twist cones.

In addition to the planning process, I also had to develop a set of rules, in writing, posted on the refrigerator so I could point to it when Alexa attempted negotiations, which was often. The rules list started fairly short, but was added to as we discovered new behaviors in trying to hide or restrict food.

1. What you are given is exactly what you need for meals and snacks. No more. No less.
2. You must eat what you are given within 1 hour. There must be nothing left in your mouth at that time.
3. There is no negotiation for meals until your weight is medically stable. The doctor will tell you when that is.
4. There is no negotiating "deals" for eating, "I'll eat this if..."
5. Someone will remain with you when you eat.
6. If you need to go to the bathroom during a meal

    a. *There must be no food or drink in your mouth, or*

    b. *Someone will go with you*

7. *If meals are not finished before we need to go somewhere:*

    a. *If it is somewhere we know you like, you must remain in the vehicle until your meal is finished (like we did before you went to school).*

    b. *If it is somewhere we know you'd rather not be, you will take your meal to the location and eat it there (like we did in church).*

8. *Every time you finish your meal in under 1 hour, you get a sticker on the calendar.*

    a. *13 stickers in one week = trip to the drive in for ice cream*

    b. *If you get stickers for all 3 meals, you get to paint a small area of your room (puzzle piece)*

    c. *If you eat a meal in 45 minutes or less, you get a "bonus" sticker (that does not count toward the 13 above). When you earn 5 of these, you can get a Webkinz.*

9. *If any meal goes over 1.5 hours, you lose technology for the next 24 hours. You may earn 30 minutes back if you get a sticker (eat in 1 hour) at the following meal.*

10. *When a meal goes over 2 hours*

    a. *Privileges already earned may be taken away — like a Webkinz.*

    b. *We will take you to the doctor's office to determine if medical attention is necessary (like IV for dehydration).*

11. *Your bedtime snack will be chosen for you if dinner is not completed before bedtime snack is scheduled. At that time, you will stay up until all food is gone.*

12. *You may pet the dog or eat outside (if someone accompanies you) if that helps you complete your meal faster.*

13. *If we determine you are too angry or emotional to talk, we will tell you that. When you are calm enough to talk, you will say "I'd like to talk."*

14. *Breakfast*
    a. *Will be chosen the night before*
    b. *You are responsible to get yourself up and going in the morning and get your breakfast.*
    c. *If breakfast isn't done, no school*

15. *If no weight gain by next appt*
    a. *Lunch at different table with para*
    b. *Lunch with secretary in office until done*
    c. *Me or Dad come in for lunch and you eat with us*

As I read these rules now, it reminds me of how tricky and manipulative an eating disorder can be. Having these rules in writing made them very clear and also made it more difficult to negotiate new things. The negotiations were regular. When she started negotiating, we could simply point to the rules. No words necessary. When we were eating, it felt like the fewer the words, the better. No misinterpretations.

These rules were the only way I could survive. Otherwise, all blame and failures felt like they were placed on me. I also put a lot of pressure on myself. The food planning probably didn't have to be that detailed. I think after a few weeks with a nutritionist, they no longer asked about meal plans. It was just about getting all the calories in. I wanted to balance as much as possible — get the calories in AND be healthy.

I was resisting junk as if that was to blame. The Mom Guilt was building. I felt a lot of pressure to cook good meals at this time. It was also a high-pressure time at work. I think, because of all the pressure, I imagined we ate more junk than I would have liked. I could have also been wondering why I was struggling when my own mom managed to work, milk cows and cook and clean when I was a kid.

I suspect when people read how much time I felt like I spent on food — 6 to 8 hours a day during the worst times — they might think I was *exaggerating. It really did take that much time to plan, prep, eat, clean up and then do it again for the next snack or meal. All of that extra time could have been used to take care of myself, have fun — who knows. I just know it was all exhausting. When I think of all that rigidity, I think it must have been hell for everyone.*

Alexa's Perspective:

There was a lot about the meal planning I didn't understand. I remember seeing these charts when the nutritionist first gave them to my mom. Seeing so many numbers laid out per day was overwhelming. Food was already hard and now it was laid out in numbers on a spreadsheet, which made the difficulty of it all even more real. Luckily, I didn't necessarily have to understand what it all meant or plan the food myself — that was mom's job. However, that didn't feel like a win either.

Though I didn't have control over the food planning process, or much else for that matter, I did enjoy getting to go over the school calendar to choose which days I liked the food, as well as the lists of food for us to help plan some meals during the week. If someone was going to be looming over me watching what I ate, I could at least try to make it so I was eating foods I kind of enjoyed.

The rules list mom created started small and grew over the course of our journey. Every time something didn't go exactly right while I was eating, mom found a way to turn what went wrong into a rule. It was as if I was trapped in a box that was gradually getting smaller and smaller. Eventually, I'd have to start thinking outside of the box.

Tangled Vines

EASTER EXPLOSION

When the kids are at Grandma and Grandpa's house, they always have cookies, cake and jars full of candy at their disposal. My parents encourage the kids to take whatever they want and tell them not to worry about what their parents say. I know this is not an intentional disrespect for our job as parents — it is just a way to show love.

I also come from the clean plate club — you must clean your plate to get dessert. The problem with this is that often, when we were kids, we did not get to choose what was on our plate. Additionally, sometimes my dad and older brother thought it was funny to put food on the plate of the person next to them; specifically, any food they knew the person didn't like. They did it as a "joke" but there were times when the "fun" turned, and we were forced to eat what was on our plate, no matter how it got there.

Easter in 2010 took place on April 4, just a couple of weeks after we started our journey at the eating disorder clinic. In the morning, we attended sunrise service and breakfast at church and survived it without incident. Then, like most years, my extended family, including my two brothers with spouses, niece and nephew, celebrated the holiday at my parents' house, about 20 minutes from where we lived.

To be honest, I did not really want to go. The diagnosis was new and I hadn't processed it yet. My family operates mostly in sarcasm or passive-aggressive "joking" and I didn't want to deal with that. I had no patience for it at that time. I didn't fully understand what we were dealing with, and how we were supposed to handle food yet. But I also knew how important the cousin relationship was — all four of the grandchildren were close in age, with Alexa being the youngest. They loved playing together and I knew I couldn't squash their precious relationships.

My Mom knew about the diagnosis, but I don't think the rest of the family did unless she told them. Meals were hard enough at home with our immediate family. Adding a few of my family's quirks into the mix was going to add to the difficulty. I was especially concerned about my family's nature and practice to tell others the solutions to their problems, even if they know nothing or have no experience with the problem. I know I am not immune, just setting the stage for all that was at play that day.

The kids usually sat against the wall — all lined up in a row. I usually sat next to Mom, who had the most open spot in the kitchen to grab things as needed. I would have preferred to sit next to Alexa to protect her from the whole "you need some of this (that you don't like)" joke. I also knew that might call more attention to Alexa and the situation, so I attempted to keep within our normal routine for the holiday.

Most of the meal went well. I was growing frustrated with the sweets Alexa was taking instead of the food I thought she should have, but I hadn't yet heard from the counselor, doctor, or nutritionist that there was good or bad food. They just wanted me to do my best to make sure Alexa got as many of the dietary requirements as possible.

Toward the end of the meal, Alexa was struggling to finish while everyone else was long done. Family members were jumping in and telling her what she needed to do. I knew that saying "just eat" wasn't one of them. No one was doing or saying anything helpful and I could feel my blood boiling.

"Just shut up! You are not helping" is what I wanted to say. From experience, I knew that wouldn't have gone well either. I was waiting for Robert to step in, perhaps and say something or even pull Alexa into another room. But he did nothing. I felt it all boil up — antagonism for my family's know-it-all position, frustration with Alexa for food choices and time, and then anger at Robert for not stepping up to be a parent. Deep inside, I was also confused and scared. With all that, the situation escalated inside me and I blew.

I told Robert we were going to leave and I said something over the table like "it would be nice if I got some help from anyone." I started packing up whatever we brought in the way of toys and asked the kids to get their coats and boots on.

I was on a rampage, totally out of control and no one dared get in my way. No one was going to tell me what to do anymore. What did they even know about any of it?

The kids and Robert begrudgingly got in the car and we headed home. I did not settle down on that 20-minute drive, ruminating and getting more and more angry. I think the kids may have been crying or angry — I don't recall. I only heard what was going on in my head. When we got home, my rampage kept coming.

I took out the garbage can and proceeded to go through every cupboard in the house, throwing away anything I felt was junk food; sweets, crackers, sugared cereal, and the list goes on. I threw out several garbage bags that day and no one could stop me. I think Robert tried a couple of times, but I wasn't hearing it. Eventually, I think everyone else went to the basement to watch a movie.

After tossing about everything in the house, I directed my attention to searching online for "appropriate" foods to replace what I had tossed. Eventually, I went to bed by myself. As a part of our next appointment at the clinic, I took time at Whole Foods and Trader Joe's where I tried to find more wholesome versions of some of the foods I had thrown out. I got the "organic" and "better" versions of goldfish, pop tarts, and chocolate grahams. I thought I could blame the food.

On the outside, I was angry. On the inside, I felt so alone and confused. I was absolutely terrified that Alexa was going to die and that I was responsible. It brings me to tears writing about it. I felt like I had not one other soul helping me then. I had no one to talk to. I did not feel like my family really supported me — as in, ask what I needed, ask how they might be able to help, ask about how appointments were going. Instead, I always felt judged.

I think some levels of resentment were building too. When Nick got diagnosed with Asperger's, I dug into the literature, attended groups, and did everything I could to learn how to parent a child on the spectrum. Robert did not do any of that. I felt left to parent by myself. Underneath, I knew I wasn't likely to get help from Robert.

There weren't any resources from the counselors, either. They did not provide me with a group of moms I could connect with or share information. I don't even recall them checking in with me — appointments focused on Alexa. I was sinking in a hole, totally alone. I was also blaming myself for everything. I really don't know what I was trying to prove. I guess it was my way to try and control the situation.

Looking back and trying to put myself in my kids' shoes, I get disgusted with myself. My dad did a lot of things that scared me as a child and I imagine this was a scary day for my kids. I did the very thing to them that I hated most as a child — the out-of-control and out-of-proportion outbursts, although sometimes they led to violence in my childhood. You never knew when they were going to show up.

I cannot take back what happened, nor the impact on my kids. I was weak that day and gave into an old behavior I had seen as a child. All I can do is hope that in sharing this story, my kids feel my deepest regrets and others will learn there are better ways to handle these things. I wish I had the strength that day to say I was not up for the holiday and stayed home.

I must grant myself a lot of compassion. It feels normal that an explosion might happen given the kind of pressure I was under. I was overwhelmed and I made mistakes. I didn't know what to do and no one was helping me. But we survived it.

Overwhelm and loneliness can do great harm. I prayed a lot back then, but it still felt very lonely. Eventually, we ended up with some key support people (angels) who came to our rescue and lessened my feelings of loneliness.

Alexa's Perspective:

Several times throughout my childhood, mom would change food preferences in some ways, whether it was getting rid of highly processed foods in our diets or switching common household staples for the organic versions of the same foods. So, while I was thinking in the back of my mind "mom is going a little crazy right now," I wasn't all that surprised. I always felt her changes and choices were a bit extreme. Some of the new versions of foods my brother and I ended up enjoying, but others we despised. Why be so stuck in getting "good" foods when the other "bad" versions we were eating were actually pleasant and easier for us to eat?

BRACELETTING FOR THE WORST

Whenever something difficult comes up in life, my mom's instinct is to learn everything she can about it to figure out the best way to overcome it. While this quality is probably quite helpful in many situations for many reasons, it was not helping me on this particular day fairly early on in my eating disorder journey.

We traveled all the way back to the eating disorder center for a conference. This was a conference where kids with eating disorders and their parents could come together to hear advice, find a "community," or just to learn more information. I was not excited about it, but I was also glad there wouldn't be any doctor's visits or other appointments like there usually were when we visited this terrible place.

We filed into a large conference room that had carpet, soft lights and chairs circled around the perimeter. There were probably about ten or so other families quietly taking their seats alongside my mom and me. There were a lot of teenage and young adult girls and their parents, a woman greeting everyone, whom I could only assume was the facilitator, and one young man with his parents. I was undoubtedly the youngest person there. A vague tension was in the air, no one certain what to feel or what to say or even what to do. We waited awkwardly for several minutes before the facilitator closed the door and welcomed us all to the conference.

For the next hour or two we listened as different individuals told their stories of struggle and recovery. Around the room I could see some holding back tears and others jotting down notes. There were a variety of different expressions, some wide eyed and glued in, others blank and distant. I could feel the inspiration in the air but, for me, most of the words were going in one ear and out the other. I appreciated the hopeful stories, but I also didn't feel connected to the conversations. I just sat quietly waiting for the end. Though I wasn't taking much of the experience in, I was glad to have no expectations to do anything or eat anything. I didn't have to talk, or eat, or work on an assignment or please anyone. I could just sit back and let my thoughts drift off.

Then the facilitator introduced the only boy in the room and his parents, and I was curious enough to tune in a little more. It turned out he was one of the people here to tell his story of recovering from an eating disorder. For whatever reason, I wasn't expecting him to be a speaker. It didn't seem common to me for boys to struggle with food. On top of that, he appeared somewhere between 18 and 20 years old, which was not someone I would expect to be so open about their eating disorder. He spoke very well; for someone so young, he seemed very mature in the way he talked about his story. He touched on the lows and the highs, and it ended with us all feeling a little more inspired than before he had started.

After he spoke to us, it was time for a brief intermission from the conference. The facilitator gave us fifteen minutes to get out of the room and go to the bathroom, grab a snack, or whatever else we needed to process or unwind. My mom said she was going to run to the bathroom and look for a snack. I noticed a group of the kids from the conference going upstairs, so I decided to follow them. We went up several flights of stairs, going past the second floor where I usually had my appointments. The girls opened the door to a different floor and started filing into the hallway. I watched several girls go into different doors down the hallway, quietly closing their doors behind them.

I wasn't sure where they were all going, but it obviously wasn't a group endeavor. I stood awkwardly near the entrance to the hallway, trying to decide what to do next. I had followed the crowd up here but hadn't really known why or where I was going. I continued slowly down the hallway. To my left, there was one of the window nooks that seemed to be everywhere in this place. There was a girl sitting with her entire body up on the window ledge, her back resting against one side of the window and her knees curled up about halfway to her chest. She looked like she was about 15 or 16, with soft facial features and earphones. As I looked closer, I noticed her fingers were twiddling with string. I didn't know what she was doing, but I thought she looked cool. I must've been staring a little longer than I intended, trying to take in the situation, because suddenly the girl made a half glance towards me.

"Hey, what's up?" I was pretty shy around new people, so I was a little nervous that maybe I had hurt her feelings by watching her, but I was glad she spoke up first.

"Hi, sorry. I just followed you all up here, I wasn't sure what to do."

"We all just came up here to our rooms during the break."

"Your rooms?"

"Yeah, we live here during treatment, so these are our bedrooms."

I glanced down the hall where all the girls had gone into their rooms, now realizing they had come up here to be alone, so I felt even more out of place. But she had started talking to me, so maybe it was ok.

"What are you doing with that string?" I asked and pointed to her hands.

"I'm making bracelets. They're like friendship bracelets I guess, but I just make them for myself when I don't have anything else to do here." As she explained, I noticed the many bracelets running halfway up her arm and was a little embarrassed I hadn't figured out what she was doing before I asked. "Do you want to make one?"

"Really?"

"Sure, I'll teach you." She reached for a bag that was filled with colored string. "What colors do you want? Maybe pick three of them to start your first one." She let me pull my three colors from the bag, then took the three pieces of string and tied them together at one end. She explained that it's basically tying the strings in rows and making more and more rows until the bracelet is finished. She looped the first string around the second string and pulled it tight up to the knot she had made earlier, which created a little knot itself. She repeated that, then moved on to loop the first string twice around the third string. Now the original second string had become the new first string, and the process could start over.

"Does that make sense? You got it from here?" She handed me the set of tied strings.

"Yeah, I think so, thanks." I sat in one of the chairs in the window nook and started working on my new bracelet. It took me a few tries to get the hang of it, but soon I was making some good progress. I looked back up to admire the bracelets covering her lower arms; they were in many different colors and were many different widths, and each one had so much character. I was happy to be here with her, and I thought she had cool style.

As we sat in silence working away, my mom suddenly appeared in the doorway with a concerned look on her face. She hurriedly walked over to me, grabbed my arm, and pulled me away from the window nook.

"I want to stay up here," I said. I'm having fun, we're making bracelets." I showed her the strings dangling from my hand.

"You shouldn't be hanging out with that girl," she said as she opened the door to the hallway and pulled me along to start heading down the stairs. I had no idea what she was talking about; I could only hope that the girl didn't hear my mom make that comment.

We went back into the conference room and soon the other families started filing back in. My mind must have been in a daze after that, because I don't remember seeing the girl come back to the conference room, or much else about what happened during the event. It seemed to fly by. Soon, my mom and I were making our way out to our car to head home. When we got into the car, I couldn't help but ask, "Why shouldn't I hang out with the girl making bracelets?"

"Those girls live there, Alexa. All the time."

"Why does that matter?" I was so confused. Who cared where we all lived?

"She is probably going to die soon, Alexa. You don't need to be talking to those types of people and getting things in your head." I was shocked. I couldn't completely process what she had just said. Why was my mom making these terrible comments? I took a moment to pause before responding.

"She was just teaching me how to make bracelets."

"Do you know why she has so many? Because that's all she has to do there. That's about the only fun thing she probably gets to do. Do you want that to be you?" I clutched the barely-started bracelet I still had and turned towards the window. I didn't have an answer to that question. I thought the girl was beautiful, creative, talented, and kind. We were just making bracelets. I saw nothing wrong with what we had been doing.

My mom and I rode in silence after that. I continued to face the window so she couldn't see the tears quietly rolling down my cheeks. I didn't even know the girl's name. What if I never saw her again? I couldn't even apologize or tell her I didn't agree with my mom. What if what my mom was saying is true, that she was dying? How would I ever know if she was ok? I felt in my heart she would be just fine, but I was swept up by a sudden fear and uncertainty. If that's what my mom thought about her, what did people think about me? Was I just someone slowly dying, that people should stay away from? All I could do was cry. And I did, the entire way home.

Mom's Perspective:

About two months into our journey, in mid-May, we were invited to attend a two-day eating disorder workshop for parents which was held at the eating disorder facility. I was happy about the opportunity because I needed to talk to some other people going through this experience. I was desperate for any tips that might help because I didn't get much for parenting tips during Alexa's appointments. Our appointments were focused on her weight and whatever happened for her during the counseling sessions. I needed information and had high expectations that I'd find some kindred souls and perhaps some new information.

The event was held on a Thursday and Friday, so we had to take off work and Alexa had to take off school. The event included education sessions and some activities. There was a little planning to do because Alexa also had an elementary concert on Thursday evening, and she had to be at school by 6:45 pm. The school was an extra 30 minutes west of our home and would be almost 2 hours in rush hour traffic. Plus, we had to get supper on the way home.

I recall entering the room and seeing a circle of chairs. We chose chairs near the window so we could catch some outside sun. People forced smiles at each other, knowing we were all very nervous to be there — and per- haps ashamed. The introductions were short and sweet, and we got down to business.

I remember being surprised that one of our speakers would be a young man, around 18, who would tell us a story about his recovery. I was curious to hear what he had to say because I was quite surprised that a male would be speaking. I'd only expected girls. While he was definitely an inspiring speaker, it struck me that his situation had to be very different from my daughter's, not just by gender but by age. She was one of the youngest people in the room, if not the youngest.

During one of the early breaks, the girls all left the room and Alexa followed. I didn't think anything of it — they seemed to know what they were doing. As I spoke to some of the other parents, it didn't take long to realize that the rest of the girls were residents there.

In-patient care.

I quickly tried to find Alexa, hoping she wasn't going places she wasn't supposed to. I found her talking to a girl and it seemed like they were having a nice conversation. I told Alexa that we should go back to the room because I didn't think she was supposed to be up there. Her temporary smile quickly dissipated, and she followed me back downstairs.

The part I remember quite vividly was at one of the breaks. Parents were asked to select a snack for their children. I think I grabbed a chewy granola bar for Alexa and a banana. One of the other couples also grabbed a banana and a granola bar and went back to their chairs and handed the snacks to their daughter (not the girl with the bracelet). She instantly got angry.

"You purposely picked out the highest calorie bar!"

From that point on, the heated exchange went on. The parents tried to keep it as low as they could, but we were nearby and could hear pretty much everything. I had seen the parents just randomly reach for a bar, not looking at the calorie count. They told her as much, but she wasn't hearing it.

They asked her to start eating the banana. She took a bite and put the rest of the banana down. For the next 15 minutes, they urged her to keep taking more bites and, at best, she got down half of the banana. I heard them threaten to not allow her to go to dance or theater, but I could see just by their body language that it was an idle threat. She knew it too. I don't remember what she said, but it was definitely in an "I dare you" tone. I recognized the fight. They never did get her to eat anything beyond the banana. They all took their seats, the girl looking smug and victorious, her parents seeming embarrassed and defeated, overwhelmed and at a loss.

We stopped at Kentucky Fried Chicken that night, one of Alexa's favorites, on the way to school for the concert. We had an hour or more to eat in the car before arriving at school. That first day had been pretty good because she had food she liked, she loved music and would be with her friend Macy that evening.

The second day, after we were home, I remember talking about some of the people at the workshop. I remember saying I wasn't sure the girl who'd struggled eating her snack with her parents was going to make it. Even if she did recover at the center, I didn't think her parents were strong enough to get her through. I don't recall the exact words I said and do admit having doubts about her recovery.

I had done my best to participate in the sessions, including a "drums alive" activity and yoga. I tried to ask questions and interact. Before I went to bed that night, I had to put my thoughts into my journal, to download. I noted that Robert had not participated in any of the activities, nor did he ask a single question while we were there. I wrote "This is not about you. If you're not going to participate, then you don't get to make decisions. Alexa learns that she doesn't have to participate either."

That was it. That's all I had to say.

ALL EYES ON ME

My life was slowly being consumed by my eating disorder. I continued to travel to the Cities for appointments roughly twice a week, my mom had new rules and meal plans for me to follow at home, and the changes even started to trickle into my school life. As part of my "treatment," my mom had asked if someone could be assigned to watch me during lunchtime.

"You can't do that! Everyone will know there's something wrong with me then, and people will make fun of me for having someone sitting with me at lunch! It's so dumb!"

"They won't sit with you; they'll just be there to keep an eye out and make sure you're eating the lunches I send with you. No one will even notice."

I didn't believe her for a second. People would notice. But I knew there wasn't any talking her out of this one. She had already called the school and they were happy to oblige.

Luckily for my mom, there was already someone assigned to be in the lunchroom to keep order and she would be happy to keep an extra close eye on me, or hold me back from class if I wasn't finished eating in time. Yippee.

The woman was a paraprofessional who usually worked with kids who had struggles in school due to disabilities, which I thought just added to my problems; now I would be grouped with the kids who were "special." I had nothing against the kids she usually worked with — my brother, Nick, had several paras growing up during school because he was diagnosed with Asperger's Syndrome and he was one of my favorite people in the world. But I knew how the other kids at school viewed the kids who had paras and that's what I was worried about. I didn't want anyone to know about my eating disorder or think differently of me.

Maybe I knew from how my brother was bullied that being associated with a para could potentially bring me the same fate. And outside of these eating problems people seemed to think I had, there was absolutely nothing wrong with me. I did amazing in school (I got all A's) and got along with most people, so there was no reason for me to be associated with a para. I was especially worried because I had just moved schools that year. While I had made some new friends, I knew it could be easy for people to form opinions of me even if they didn't fully know me or the situation.

There was only one person in school who knew about my eating disorder stuff, and that was Macy.

Macy and I met on the very first day of school; she sat in front of me in our fourth-grade class. As the first class was getting started, her reddish-brown bob of hair in front of me turned around to reveal the biggest smile. Macy introduced herself and welcomed me to the school, and I could tell that she had the warmest, most genuine heart. I somehow knew we would be the best of friends. From that day on, we partnered up for assignments, planned activities together, and took turns spending the night at each other's houses. Our families also bonded through our friendship. I think that's how Macy eventually found out about my eating disorder — through my mom talking to her mom. I was very hush-hush about my eating disorder. Though I didn't care if Macy knew, I wasn't one to go around sharing the information; I wasn't even sure if I believed it anyway. My mom, on the other hand, wasn't shy about letting people know.

We never bluntly talked about it — how she knew or what she thought about it — but you could tell Macy was mindful when it came to situations with me and food.

Most notably, there was a day at lunch that I was struggling to finish my food. The lunchroom para (who I had quickly come to despise) walked over and dug her hands into my lunch bag. She fingered through the contents and of course spotted my half eaten peanut butter and jelly that I had tried to hide under my empty applesauce and pudding cups. She wouldn't have even noticed if she had left my stuff alone; I didn't think she really had the right to be digging around in my personal property.

"You need to finish your sandwich." She picked it up to show me like I didn't already know what was in there. I snatched it from her hands so it wasn't dangling in my face.

"Ok," I quickly whisper-snapped at her. Usually, I would put up more of a fight, but I didn't want to draw attention to the interaction. Why did she have to be so obvious? So much for "no one noticing" like my mom thought. It's not exactly typical to have someone inspecting your lunch bag and instructing you what to eat. My friends at the table didn't seem to take much notice through their chatter though and, luckily, my quick remark at least got her to walk away and scan over the rest of the lunchroom.

My friends and I chatted and ate for a few more minutes before they all stood up at once, signaling they were done. I made a glance back to the para to see if I could walk with them to sneak past her, but her gaze was fixated on me. I stayed sitting and stared at my lunch bag, desperately thinking of what to do or say. I could feel my heart rate start to rise.

"We're heading outside for recess, aren't you coming?" All eyes fell to me. I was devastated and didn't know what to do.

"No, I'm not done eating yet," was all I could manage to say. A few eyebrows raised and the group stood there awkwardly for a moment, as if they were waiting to see if I was kidding. I wished I was. As they were about to leave to dump their trays and abandon me, Macy sat back down.

"You guys go ahead; I'm going to stay here with Alexa."

She plopped her tray back down next to me and started a new conversation like nothing had happened. I watched as the rest of my friends made their way outside to recess, and I couldn't help but wonder why Macy didn't go with them.

Why would she miss out on her recess?

I was dying to go outside. Our friends had looked a little confused at her decision too, but Macy didn't waver one bit. Even though I was confused, I was also extremely relieved. I could almost feel the metaphorical weight physically being lifted off my shoulders. Now I wouldn't have to sit awkwardly alone, and I knew I was sitting with someone who wouldn't judge me.

We continued to talk like nothing had happened. It seemed like the smallest thing — sitting with someone for a few extra minutes — but to me, that small act was everything in that moment. I felt like I should say something to her, to thank her, but between processing the situation and the mix of adrenaline and relief flowing through me, the words wouldn't come. Instead, I put on a smile and kept up the small talk while I managed to take the last few bites of my sandwich.

I hoped my gratefulness would pass through the air to her, unspoken but there in spirit. I like to think that it did, because as we strolled back to class like any other day, there was a newness between us. A newness that felt as though we could stand side by side and face the world, as if nothing could break us apart. I couldn't believe how lucky I was to have such an amazing friend.

Mom's Perspective:

Shortly after the diagnosis and getting the nutritional plan in place, I made an appointment to talk to the school counselor. I was going to need her on my side.

I needed Alexa to eat her lunch at school. It was already tough enough when we were together to eat; there was no way I could jam any more calories into breakfast or dinner. If someone from the school couldn't watch her at lunch, I was going to have to do it myself. And that would require another 1.5 hours (45 min each way) to drive to school to do it and more extended leave from work. I know there was no way Alexa would want me there for the unwanted attention it would attract.

I met with the school counselor to provide a situational update on Alexa's diagnosis and to talk about how I might get the school's support in this effort. I mentioned the pact that the nurse said she had overheard and that she might be on the watch for continued discussion there. I asked how I might go about having someone watch Alexa to make sure she ate her lunch every day. I said that if it wasn't someone from the school then I would have to come myself and I didn't think that was a great idea. The counselor understood the situation and agreed to be the person in the lunchroom as much as possible. She said she would work with some others when she might be called out or unavailable. She said it would be an opportunity to talk to some of the kids outside of the office and that might even make it easier for them to come to her. She said it wouldn't be a problem at all.

I could see the sincerity and empathy in her eyes. She felt exactly like someone I could trust to help care for Alexa. Before coming to the meeting, I had been anxious about the possibility of no one being able to take on the job. I was deeply relieved to have someone on my side — my first teammate, so to speak.

I asked the counselor to do her best to not give away that I had spoken to her about Alexa's situation. I also asked her to keep it on a need-to-know basis. She agreed that she would only tell those who absolutely needed to know.

I could have taken Alexa home from school that day, but I decided to sneak out before anyone else noticed. I didn't want her to know I was there talking to anyone about her situation. I made it out of the building, to the parking lot and out of the area without too many people even taking notice. Whew — task complete.

I think there were only a handful of times when the counselor called to say that Alexa had struggled with lunch. Sometimes she would encourage Alexa to finish and other times she made the decision not to push. I sensed she was doing her best to fulfill our agreement, but also feeling like she was doing what was best for Alexa during the school day. There were times when Alexa was having a bad day in other ways and Alexa came to talk. She never shared what they talked about, but we did our best to keep communication lines open. I appreciated everything she was doing for us.

A WEEKEND TO FORGET

My parents had a seasonal camper on Red Lake in northern Minnesota. The year of Alexa's diagnosis, they invited us up for Memorial Day Weekend. The week before our visit, issues just kept piling up.

On several occasions during that week and the week before, instead of being a parent, Robert left all the hard things for me. For instance, we had a rule that said Alexa could only take music on the bus on Friday and had to earn so many stickers during the week. Instead of just saying no when Alexa asked and pointing to the rule, he came down to my office to ask me if she could take music on the bus. So, of course, when we went back up it was "Mom said no." I felt so alone in the job of parenting and I resented that.

Another morning, Alexa was struggling to get food down and ended up needing to be driven to school instead of taking the bus. This wasn't a usual thing. At that same time, someone called for hay. Robert baled the nearby ditches and sold the hay throughout the year. He asked if I could take Alexa to school even though he knew I had to get to work and he could have easily asked the customer for a later time. I think people think that working from home is just a casual thing without discipline or schedule. I was very committed to my work and knew my most productive times were in the morning. At that point, I knew nothing was going to change. He was not going to help. In fact, he would hinder. He was focused on himself.

The evening before we were set to leave to go camping with my parents, I was really angry. I asked Robert to name a single thing he was doing to help Alexa and he could not name one. At that point I told him to stay home from the trip. I already had two kids to deal with, I did not need any more counteractive behaviors and more stress. He didn't really argue with me, at least.

The drive up was pretty quiet. I just had some music on. The kids watched movies and played their Nintendo DS games. We didn't talk much.

I was still stewing about having to do this alone. When we arrived, we were greeted with a smile and treats from my mom.

I think all three of us slept on the pullout bed in the camper because both the kids were small enough. It was kind of fun doing sleepover-style. Plus, I was taking a sleep aid by then, so any movement or noise didn't really affect me.

As usual, Grandma cooked great food and had all the cookies and other treats the kids liked on hand. We often don't struggle as much with food around her. I was also learning to accept that there were no good or bad foods. Alexa needed calories and she needed food she liked. Extra goodies from Grandma did not hurt our cause.

We did some fishing off the dock and in the canal near the campground. I have this picture of Alexa with a fish that, for me, is the epitome of her eating disorder. She is smiling with the fish held out in front of her (by my dad) and she is leaning over it. Her head is disproportionately larger than her body and it always makes me sad that this even happened to us.

Anyway, the reason my parents camped on Red Lake is they like to fish, mostly for our state fish, the walleye. My dad wanted to take us out to the lake. Both kids were kind of hesitant to go, but got life jackets on and got in the boat. The boat was big enough to hold about four adults. No one sat on the front seat until the boat had settled out on the lake. We also needed heavy jackets because May in northern Minnesota can be pretty chilly — snow is not out of the question.

As we tooled through the canal and around a bend where we could see the lake, I could see the swells rising with plenty of white caps. I suggested that we turn around and I could see the terror in both kids' faces. I held Alexa while my stubborn dad kept going.

The kids started crying.

We weren't very far from the canal, out in the waves, and Dad decided to throw out the walleye hooks — these are large hooks that you pull slowly through the water. He got them in and was trolling along watching behind the boat.

I could see he was about to cross over the lines coming from another boat. I yelled at him to stop but, as usual, he was not listening to me or caring what I had to say and he kept going. At that point, the people in the other boat started yelling and he finally got it. But it was too late. One of the lines from the other boat came flying out of the water and the big walleye hook just missed my mom's head. The kids were in a panic and I was furious. After that, he finally headed back in. As soon as the boat pulled up to the dock, my kids jumped out and took off for the camper. I stomped back too.

There wasn't anything else to say to my dad at that point either, because he doesn't listen to me anyway. He was never going to admit he did anything wrong. So, I spent the night doing my best to stay present with the kids while ignoring anything else he had to say (I am stubborn too).

What I thought would be a little escape for us from the stress of home was just another reminder of how little support men provided in my life. This situation only aggravated what I was experiencing with Robert. My thoughts went back to my own relationship, and getting little or no support for what Alexa was dealing with.

All I could think about was how grateful I was that I had someone ready to help me the following week — hopefully this was where I could obtain some support and relief.

On the drive home, we talked a bit about my dad and his inability to think about others. I was hopeful my kids would understand what I had to deal with my whole life and have compassion. I don't think they understood at the time and that is to be expected.

I was apprehensive about what would happen when we got home. To be honest, I didn't want to talk about it. I had a child to save, and that's where I had to focus my limited energy.

I wish I had the skills at the time to say what I needed and how Robert needed to show up. Or find a place to help build up his ability to be a parent, beyond babysitting. We both grew up in German families where gender roles were clearly defined — no exceptions. I had refused these roles and was trying to change amid everything happening with Alexa — it didn't work.

Alexa's Perspective:

I enjoyed fishing off the dock in the quiet canal. Grandpa had taken us fishing before and I was glad he shared his hobby with us. However, I get motion sickness very easily. I didn't much enjoy boats or waves because they instantly made me feel queasy. Since the canal did not have any waves and the water seemed calm, when grandpa offered to take us on the boat, I was ok with giving it a try.

When we rounded the corner, I could see the large waves and my stomach dropped. I told my family I didn't want to go out and we should turn around. But grandpa really wanted to fish out on the lake, so he kept going. The boat began to rock harder and harder as we went further into the depths of the lake.

For whatever reason, as I sat crying and begging for us to go back to shore, an overwhelming feeling of my dad's missing presence swept over me. Maybe because dad couldn't swim and also would've been uncomfortable in this situation. Maybe because I could feel the growing tension within our family and sadness that I could do nothing about it, just as I could do nothing about this situation. But I missed him. All I wanted was for him to be there. For this to end.

I remember the hook flying and the other boat getting upset at us, which luckily escalated the situation enough for us to turn around — finally. Unfortunately, I think we were all feeling defeated at this point though. For the rest of the trip, we all just went through the motions. We still had some fun, but there was an unease in the air amongst us all.

DOCTOR'S INTERVENTION

One of the hardest days of my life occurred on June 4, 2010. It was the last day of the school year. It should have been a celebration. The day started out okay for the first twenty minutes, but then went downhill from there.

Alexa stopped eating and I reminded her about the rules — if she didn't complete her meal within one hour she would lose electronics. She wrote on a piece of paper that we don't listen to her. That was partially true, I suppose, since much of the time we were talking and negotiating with the eating disorder. I made the mistake of saying we weren't going to talk about this. I attempted to remain calm and keep reminding her of her choices. She could eat and go to school or not eat and stay home.

Eventually, I asked if she'd like to talk to someone else and she decided to speak with the school counselor. Thankfully, she was at school when we called. The counselor told Alexa that it is impossible to speak with someone when they are so upset because their brain isn't working right. Alexa agreed to finish eating on the way to school. I think she just needed some reassurance that there were others who could help when I couldn't.

The kids arrived back home from school just after noon because it was an early dismissal day. Nick came into the house and said Alexa was mad that there was no dog food. She was in her room pouting and added that she was mad she wouldn't have access to the computer that day. I got lunch out and the situation continued to get worse. She virtually gave up trying to eat after about a half hour.

I'm not sure why, but we moved to her room after the first hour and she proceeded to spew all her anger: I lied, we don't care, we don't listen, she might as well be dead, just pull my brains out, along with some swearing. I sat in the room on a chair with my iPod and a book while she kept getting angrier. I had to stick to the rules and reminded her that after 1.5 hours she would lose computer access another day. She wasn't even close at that point, so I said if she didn't finish in 2 hours, we'd have to go to the doctor's office.

At that point she stripped off her clothes and also stripped everything from the bed. She kicked and banged the walls so hard the lights flickered. She curled herself up in a tiny ball in the corner of the room as tight as she could. I asked Robert to stand by the door while I called the clinic.

Once I had an appointment, I also called my then-boss's wife, who often served as our company nurse in times of need. I sensed that a medical professional wasn't going to be able to do anything from afar, but she was my first line of defense to reach out to.

She calmly asked questions to help me settle down and focus. Ultimately, she told me to go with what my gut was telling me. My gut was telling me that if we took Alexa in and I could convince the doctor to threaten an IV or needles in some way, maybe taking blood, that would "knock" her out of it. She hated needles and I hoped it would work.

My boss's wife also suggested reaching out to the eating disorder clinic, so I did that next. I was able to reach Alexa's case worker and Alexa agreed to talk briefly. The case worker didn't tell me for sure if it would be good to go to the doctor or not, so I decided we would follow through on going to the doctor.

I went to tell Nick that he would be going to Grandma's house across the road and that we needed to take Alexa to the doctor because she was sick. I started crying and he did a little too, but managed to wipe the tears from MY eyes.

This was a beautiful gift coming from a child on the autism spectrum and I cherish it. I could see in his eyes that he was worried too. I told him we'd get some special time with him when we returned.

Robert took Nick over to his mom and dad's house and Alexa got dressed to go in. I seem to recall we had to carry her to the car and buckle her in.

She still hadn't finished her lunch when we arrived at the clinic at 3pm. We took the food in with us which, at that point, also included afternoon snack. Because this was a short notice appointment, we had to take the first *doctor available. When we were told who the doctor would be, I admit, I didn't have much hope. Dr. X was an older male doctor and I assumed he wouldn't really understand or be able to help much. Little did I know what was about to happen.*

When the doctor arrived, I informed him that she was out of control, and we didn't know what else to do. I explained we were amid an eating disorder and some treatment. Alexa's rage had switched to quiet anxiety by then. Upon quick examination, the doctor said her blood pressure was a little high and that it could be dehydration. With a look of slight anguish on his face, he asked Robert and I if we'd be willing to come to his office to chat. This had never happened before and my gut ached. I was worried he was going to suggest a mental health facility for a night somewhere.

As it turned out, he had a daughter who passed away after a long battle with her own eating disorder. Apparently, they started the process at age 15. He showed us some pictures on the small cork board to the side of his desk. He pointed to a picture of his daughter around age 15 and then another after a stint at an eating disorder clinic in Arizona. Finally, he pointed to a third picture of a very frail and weak looking young woman on a hospital bed. He told us that was his daughter about a week before she died — at age 23. He said they weren't strong enough to help save her and that he wished they'd been tougher on her early on. He told us we needed to be strong.

We sat in silence for a moment. I couldn't react to him and his loss, not in the state of mind I was in at the time. I felt like Robert was hit emotionally for the first time (at least that I saw). I wasn't distraught; I suspect the initial reaction was less appropriate than "I'm sorry for your loss." I remember feeling a boost of power — oddly enough as if his strength was indeed passed to me. I felt sad as well as grateful for his willingness to share. I don't care if his sharing somehow broke doctor/patient code because I needed to hear it that day.

What I heard is that I (and we) must be more vigilant.

I explained Alexa's fear of needles. We agreed to threaten her with an IV for the next day if things didn't improve. We went back into the room;

Alexa had been crying and I could see she was worried about us leaving the room. Dr. X did a little more checking and then told her what might happen. He'd let her go for now but passed on the warning. It worked. You could tell that she was fearful of us following up and it appeared to be the shock she needed because she finished her snack in the car on the way home. The fight was not over, but we gained a new ally.

We stopped to get something to drink. I also decided to pick up a timer that could sit next to her while she was eating so it didn't have to be me informing her — which always added to her aggravation. She had calmed down and was becoming a bit more of her bright self on the way home.

We stopped to get Nick and proceeded to play with their younger cousins who had been to grandma's house as well. We got home around 5pm and Alexa decided to go to her room. We were all exhausted.

But of course, it wasn't long before we'd be at supper again. I wanted to hit it a little early in case there was another incident. Thankfully, we made it through by playing some games while we ate. Alexa would get a little frustrated with losing. However, we also had some good laughs. In fact, the kids ended up doing some SpongeBob routine (one of Nick's favorite shows) and he went into that deep belly laugh — of course, you can't resist doing the same. He was in tears he was laughing so hard. I think some of it was from the enormous relief that everything was okay.

That evening, I reflected on Nick's beautiful gesture of wiping away my tears before we left for the clinic. It made me think that it might be worth having him come to a counseling session to better understand what was going on. Eventually, I think he did join us for a session or two.

When Alexa recovered, I wrote Dr. X a note, thanking him immensely for the gift he (and his daughter) gave us that day. Today, I could still walk to that room in that office and point to the wall that once held the pictures of a young life gone too soon. I hope in some way, her life lives through ours. While it was one of the worst days of my life, it was also a blessed day.

Alexa's Perspective:

Peas.

The meal holding me back was not, in fact, a whole meal. It was peas. Through my eating disorder, I struggled with certain foods because of their texture, making them hard to swallow. If I could not chew and swish them in my mouth enough to swallow them like liquid, I really struggled. Peas, while being relatively soft, have a thick skin that doesn't break down (to liquid) easily. So, I wasn't just throwing a fit to cause a fight. I was struggling to actually get the food down. Believe it or not, that was just as frustrating for me as it probably was for mom.

But no one asked me about that. No one was willing to listen to why I was struggling. They saw defiance and decided to fight back with punishment tactics.

To be honest, I didn't think mom would follow through. She had threatened to take me to the doctor or to the eating disorder clinic and drop me off to stay awhile before. We had never gone. It was unrealistic. Until this day.

I didn't eat as we drove because I still assumed that we would drive, get to the parking lot, and mom would realize she can't just take me to a doctor for something as simple as me not finishing a pile of peas. But we marched into the lobby plate in hand, and that's when my stomach sank. She wasn't messing around this time; she had officially gone bonkers. Doom took over. Suddenly, I could picture the nurses standing over, each holding down a limb as they poked me repeatedly with needles. (This may seem dramatic, but they had done it plenty of times before when I had other medical issues that caused them to take my blood about once a month).

I tried to understand what was happening but couldn't. How could one little pile of peas mean I needed all of this medical madness? Even when they tried to say I was dehydrated, it didn't make sense. Peas had nothing to do with my hydration. You want me to drink some stuff? More than happy to. Problem solved. None of it made sense, and there was nothing I could do about it. Because I was just a kid. A kid with a problem.

PANCAKES AT CHURCH

The wrath of my mom's eating disorder treatment schemes may have followed me all the way to school, but there was one place I figured it would never reach and that was church. My family had gone to the same church my entire life, a Lutheran church in a small town about 15 minutes from our house. And there were lots of reasons for my eating disorder to check itself at the door.

For one, we had community there. We have always been particularly close with my pastor and his family. They lived about ten minutes down the road from where I grew up and were more than just church friends, they were practically family. Pastor's two daughters babysat my brother and me when we were little, my parents helped out on Pastor's farm or at church events. Pastor even helped my dad build our house when I was just over one year old. We were also friends with a lot of the other members of our church — my dad knew practically everyone in the area — so I figured there was no way my mom would make a scene with all this eating disorder nonsense at church, right? We wouldn't want all those people to think poorly of us.

Judgements had already been placed upon our family over the years due to my brother's autism. Growing up, my brother struggled with social interactions that came easy to most other kids. He never wanted to engage in small talk with people at our church and, after a few attempts from my mom to make him participate in the annual Christmas program, his nervous fidgeting and endless complaints about the whole thing finally convinced my mom to let him silently pass out bulletins instead. The other adults in our church didn't understand; they just thought my brother was being rude and my parents were caving into a pre-teen's whims. They were wrong about the whole thing but, nonetheless, people didn't seem to have the most positive views of our family. We wouldn't want to add more imperfection to the mix with some silly arguments about my eating.

Plus, I already knew people at church were making judgements about my size. There were several older ladies that made it their deal to "joke" about my body as a sort of backwards compliment. There was one time when my parents stopped at a table to chit chat with a group of older ladies that one of them reached out and pinched my arm and gave it a few squeezes. "You need to put some meat on those bones," she told me. The next time she might say, "you're just a little twig." I knew they were trying to use them as a compliment to say I was skinny (and they wished they could be), but it just made me self-conscious. I couldn't help that my body was built with a smaller figure. So, when I started treatment for my eating disorder, the last thing I wanted was for them to think I actually was lacking "meat on my bones." I didn't want to prove them right. Because they weren't. I was fine just the way I was.

My entire family had reasons to avoid tarnishing our reputation, so one Sunday morning when I was struggling to finish breakfast, I figured the ticking clock leading up to us leaving for church would provide me another eating disorder battle win. My dad had whipped up some chocolate chip pancakes, which happened to be my favorite breakfast. The problem was that he flopped three pancakes on my plate when I only wanted two.

I was upset, but I figured if I drew out the process of eating the first two pancakes, the only option would be to leave the third behind and make our way to worship the Lord. Genius. I took slow bites, one chocolate chip in each, and felt myself getting fuller and fuller as I neared the end of the second pancake. I glanced toward the clock — only 10 minutes left until we had to leave, and I wasn't even dressed for church yet. My plan was working perfectly.

My mom walked into the kitchen and her eyes were instantly drawn to my plate. One and one fourth of a pancake sat soaking in syrup that was starting to harden around the plate. "Alexa, you have to eat those."

"I have to get dressed still, it's almost time to go."

"Then go and get dressed, but you're eating those pancakes." She seriously overestimated how much time we had before we needed to leave. No problem. I'd just prolong putting on my clothes and brushing my teeth.

After carefully examining my closet for the perfect outfit, fiddling with each clothing item before putting it on, and being sure to spend the full recommended two minutes brushing my teeth, it was time to go. I gave my plate an "oh darn" look as I passed it by on my way to the garage. Sweet, sweet victory.

As I swung the door open ready to make my exit, my mom came storming into the kitchen.

"Where do you think you're going? Take that plate with you, you're finishing those pancakes." She grabbed the plate and thrust it toward me. I refused to take it.

"We can't take pancakes to church."

"Oh yes we can, I said you're finishing those pancakes so you can bring them with you." She extended the plate to me again and waited until I took it from her.

I ripped the plate from my mom's hands, hoping it would send the pancakes flying to the ground and leave my mom with no choice but to forget about this crazy idea. Unfortunately, due to the solidifying syrup, they stayed put. I was furious. There was no way I was going to eat my breakfast during church; it would be so obvious, everyone would notice. We always sat towards the front of the church, about five pews back from the front, a perfect spot for people to watch you from behind without you even knowing.

As we drove, the plate sat on my lap untouched. There was still hope that mom would get to church and realize what an obnoxious thing it would be to bring food into church. We pulled into the parking lot, and when the vehicle came to a halt my mom turned to face me from around the headrest. Her face was already prepared with a look of disappointment spread all over it. She simply turned around, stepped out of the car, and opened my door.

"Grab the plate and let's go."

"You're not seriously going to make me take this into church? I'm not sitting in front of the whole church eating my food!"

"We can sit in back, but you're eating it all." She was out of her mind and I was livid. I got out of the car, threw my seat belt behind me, and left the plate on the back seat. My mom grabbed the plate and we all walked to the front doors of the church.

A man and woman stood smiling in the entryway to the sanctuary of the church holding bulletins with today's service information. My dad greeted them and took a bulletin, and he and my brother went to our normal pew at the front of the church, but my mom and I took the entry to the dining room instead.

The wall between the sanctuary and the dining room was basically a sliding curtain, and it was open, so we could still see into the sanctuary but we were sitting behind the pews instead of in them. My mom practically tossed the plate onto one of the tables and told me to sit down and start eating. A few people turned around to see what was happening. I was so embarrassed and ashamed.

I quickly averted my eyes from theirs, hoping if I looked away maybe they wouldn't see me. My eyes fell to my half-eaten plate of pancakes. At this point, the pancakes were cold and soggy, and the dark brown syrup was hardened to the plate — unspreadable and unusable. I knew no one else would find this plate of food even remotely appealing, but my mom was obviously not backing down and was going to make me eat it, no matter how unappetizing it looked. I could practically feel it going down my throat like a brick. My head was spinning, trying to think of a way to make this end, to get out of this horrible mess, but every plan I could conjure was thwarted by either the notion of making a scene or my mom catching me being sneaky.

Pastor walked into the sanctuary and centered himself in front of the pews as the church bell outside rhythmically chimed to signal the start of service. He greeted the congregation and started making announcements just like any other Sunday. For me, it was no longer any other Sunday at church, it had turned into hell. I hoped Pastor wouldn't notice half of my family sitting up front while I was back here looking like a loser who couldn't eat a stupid pancake. Tears silently rolled down my cheeks as I lifted a small bite to my mouth and forced it down. I glanced up to my mom, who stood beside me with a blank expression watching the front as the organist started playing the first song of the day. I couldn't understand why she felt ok doing this. It was embarrassing for all of us, not to mention it caused more hurt than good in my eyes.

By the end of church an hour later, I had barely managed to finish the last bites on my plate. I felt like I was those soggy, sticky pancakes as people started walking back to the dining room for coffee hour, throwing confused glances my way. I assumed they were disgusted with me like I was with my pancakes. We left the plate where it was and joined the rest of my family to sit and chat for coffee hour. My mom talked on as if nothing had happened, and I was torn between hating that we were just ignoring all of this and hoping no one would bring it up. It made me realize, if I couldn't find solace in the house of God, there must not be any place my eating disorder couldn't reach. My life and my battle with food were starting to look more and more hopeless. But I wasn't giving up, not yet.

Mom's Perspective:

It was about two months or less into our eating disorder journey and I was starting to get a real sense for what the eating disorder was capable of. It was a Sunday morning and Robert made some chocolate chip pancakes for the kids while I got ready for church. This worked out well because he could get them started and I would be ready to go and make sure Alexa finished.

I could tell she was dabbling along as usual but not super stressed out. She still had her pajamas on and had to get her teeth and hair brushed and get dressed to go. With about 20 minutes left before we had to go, I told Alexa to go get dressed and then we'd keep working on the pancakes. I had to make sure she swallowed the bite she had in her mouth before she left the kitchen island. She took her sweet time getting dressed in her room and then headed to the bathroom. As she was taking time in there, I peaked in to see what she was doing, and she was brushing her teeth. I started to sense what she was up to — keep plugging slowly and she won't have to finish.

I nagged her a few times, and she didn't move. When she finally did come out, there was only a few minutes left before she had to leave. She sat down and took one bite and then set the fork down. Robert and Nick started moving toward the garage to get in the van, so Alexa started to follow. I told her she could take the pancakes along and work on them while we drove. I picked up the plate and fork and handed it to her.

We got in the van and started heading south. I told her she would have to finish the pancakes one way or another. She took a small bite or two as we drove the 20 minutes to church, but there was at least three-quarters of a pancake left.

As we got out, Alexa was going to leave the plate behind. I told her we were bringing it along and that we'd go in the kitchen door so we could sit in the fellowship hall until she was done. At this point, Robert begged me not to make her do it. That made me even more pissed off. I felt like he was more worried about how he'd look to the people at church than the survival of our daughter. I said she had to finish it and that was it.

We were somewhat active in the church. I served on the church council and organized our church's fundraiser one year. Robert regularly helped with set up and clean up at events, along with other general building and outside projects. We also helped serve coffee hour when it was our turn during the year. We regularly sat close to the front because when the kids were small, one of the older couples in the church said that when their kids were small it helped to sit up front so they could all see. That seemed to keep their attention more and I thought it was a great idea. The kids aren't super rambunctious, but I did notice a shift when we moved from the back of the church to more toward the front.

I didn't want to fully embarrass Alexa by making her take the plate up front, which is why we went in the back door and sat in the fellowship hall. Outside of the major holidays, the sliding curtains between the church and the fellowship hall were normally closed, but this day they happened to be open. I kind of liked that so I could still hear the service while keeping an eye on Alexa.

A few heads turned backward to see us, but I wasn't really paying attention. I didn't care what people thought of it and I was quite certain no one would ask. And if they did, I was prepared to say that we were just having a bad day and leave it at that.

Alexa sat at the table and very slowly ate the rest of her pancakes. It took her nearly the entire service to finish, but she did. The service ended and people started piling back into the fellowship hall for refreshments and snacks. There were cookies and Kool-Aid for the kids to grab before Sunday School. Nick came back and grabbed a snack and drink. Alexa just grabbed a drink and they both headed off to be with their groups.

I took the plate to the kitchen to clean it off, ran it out to the minivan and came back in for refreshments myself. Robert and I joined a few others at a table and there was no further discussion. Pastor had noticed us and came to check with me if everything was okay. I thanked him and said yes, that it was just a setback and we'd be okay.

HELP HAS ARRIVED

I already had experience dealing with a deep unknown of parenting when Alexa's older brother, Nick, was diagnosed with Asperger's Syndrome when he was only five. We started with some speech issues at age three, which eventually led us to the autism spectrum. I remember it taking almost three years from the start of Kindergarten to get him to understand he couldn't always be the first in line. Thankfully, he had a full-time paraprofessional, Kris, who served as his aid through fourth grade, when our small rural school closed.

Kris was such a blessing to our family, helping us all navigate the difficulties brought on by Nick's needs. We had established such a great relationship. It didn't take long for her to come to mind when I was trying to figure out how I could get some assistance.

Paraprofessionals are used to working with behavioral issues. This was important because eating disordered individuals become masters at manipulating and hiding. They pick food apart to make it look like they ate, try to make tradeoffs, saying "if you let me do X, I'll eat that later." They insist they have to go to the bathroom and will seek out any small place to throw food. I know how hard Kris had to work with Nick on his social skills and flexibility, so I assumed she could do a similar job with Alexa. I suspect that Alexa wasn't thrilled at the idea of being with Kris because she knew it would be hard to manipulate her.

I'd contacted Kris via email with a brief explanation of what was happening and to see if she had any interest in helping out. She wanted to know more, so we set a date to meet at the local pub to discuss. I asked for most working days, but I knew that might not be realistic considering summer was time off from school and a much-needed break for all teachers and school staff.

I know how much she enjoyed working with Nick and she'd expressed how much she'd missed him at the end of the last school year. So, it was great to see the look of excitement on her face at the prospect of a continued relationship. I didn't have anyone else to turn to; if she would have declined, I would have been devastated. I desperately needed some relief. I looked back on some of my journal entries and wrote how exhausted I was multiple times during these months. When she agreed to help, I felt a sense of relief come over me. I had one more layer of hope that we could get through this.

We decided that Kris would take the kids from around 10am to as late as 4pm on Tuesday, Wednesday and Thursday each week. This allowed me to get a break from one of the meals, as well as get some work done. As a paraprofessional, I knew she had the skills needed to deal with unique behaviors presented by a variety of children. Plus, she was both encouraging and strong. She was the perfect balance of compassion and consistency. I needed all those things for Alexa.

Each day, while the kids ate breakfast, I packed lunches and snacks. They were ready when Kris came to pick them up. She lived less than ten miles away and had agreed to pick them up and take them out during that time. Not only did I get relief, but the kids had the opportunity for mini field trips, excursions and crafts all summer.

The pool was about 25 miles away, so we got a family pool pass and they spent many days there. Sometimes they played mini golf or frisbee golf. Kris took them to places like the local wildlife sanctuary, the local history museum and the county fair. They even did a few scavenger hunts and other games at the local Walmart. The attention was distracted away from the eating disorder as much as possible.

Kris and I would check in at the end of most days. She'd tell me how the day went, although I often already knew by their attitudes when they walked in the door. Many days were good, and some were struggles. Kris would describe the struggles, along with any strategies she may have implemented during the day — sometimes a little negotiation about when food would be eaten. Some days we just had to chalk it up to a bad day and move forward with the next.

Most mornings when the kids left with Kris, I'd experience a huge sense of relief. My whole body took a breath and a pause. Those portions of the middle of the day were joyous breaks from the pressure. At least early in the disorder, my body was fully tense most days, not knowing when either of us were going to explode (or maybe implode). When Kris had the kids, I could do what I wanted without worry — even if it was just an extra cup of tea in the sunroom or on the porch to decompress after a rough morning. Most of the time, I could just stay on top of my work — at least enough to survive the current project.

When I was traveling for work (which I still managed to do, but only because I had Kris to help me) Kris explained that Alexa would sometimes be extra depressed. I don't remember that — probably part of the overwhelm. I just always worried when I wasn't home because I didn't know what she would do. But Kris said when she talked to me on the phone it usually helped. I know that Alexa and I were intimately tied in this struggle. I contributed both to the struggle and to the recovery.

Every day verified for me that I could not have found anyone better to take on this unique job. I had no one else I would have trusted to handle all the techniques used to avoid eating by those with eating disorders.

When I asked Kris to recall how the summer went for her, she described how, at times, Nick was the one to encourage Alexa. Because of his Asperger's, I often felt like he wasn't paying attention — less eye contact, not looking over at me when I was talking. In reality, he probably understands the problem and Alexa's struggle more than anyone. He knew that adults often misunderstand what is going on with children, like we did with him. I think how they interacted during this time is why they are still so close today.

I seriously think Alexa and I would both be six feet under if it wasn't for Kris. She was the only direct help I had to get through the situation — the only person. Even though she didn't have direct experience with an eating disorder, she understood how I was feeling and how she could support me.

On top of the amazing work Kris did for us over the summer, she delivered an extra gift in the way of a scrapbook filled with pictures of all of their summer adventures. We have a permanent reminder of the gift she gave — and still gives — us. When I look at it, I feel incredibly blessed to have a person, an angel, like Kris who got us all through one of the most difficult times in our lives. I also realize how incredibly privileged I am to have been able to afford the help.

Alexa's Perspective:

To say I was not looking forward to an entire three months with Kris was an understatement. Kris entered our lives as support for Nick and had been working with him for years. And that's all this would be — a summer for Nick.

When we were younger — me in kindergarten and Nick in first grade — I distinctly remember an experience I had with Kris. A bunch of kids were outside playing kickball, so Nick and I joined, ending up on opposite teams. Most of the game went smoothly, but towards the end Nick and I got into an argument at home plate. I can't remember who was the runner and who was the catcher, but one of us thought it was a safe play while the other thought it was out.

As our voices raised, I could see Nick's face turning red with anger. It escalated quickly and he lashed out and bit my arm. I was never one to turn down a fight when I knew I had the upper hand (and I did with Nick). So, I reached out, grabbed his shoulder and gave him a good scratch. I had pretty sharp nails and a talent for gnarly scratches, so it cut him fairly deep. He immediately started crying and ran up the hill — to none other than Kris. I followed after him, ready to share my side of the story. Nick had very obviously started it. He was the one who took it too far. However, to my utter shock, when I got there Kris scolded me. How could I possibly scratch my brother like that? How could I possibly hurt sweet, innocent Nick? I explained that he bit me first, so I had to defend myself. Kris was taking none of it, I should know better. Nick never got in trouble.

So, when mom said we'd be spending the summer with Kris, I dreaded it. The last thing I needed was another person to not understand me and choose sides against me. She didn't like me. I didn't like her. This wasn't going to go well.

The first few weeks I held up some defiance. I didn't want to cave into her fake attempts at relating to me. But it didn't take long for me to loosen up a bit. Kris included us in planning what we would do during the week and it was always a mix of things Nick would like and things I would like. Retail store scavenger hunt for Nick, craft day for me, pool day for both of us. As time went on, it seemed the playing field was a little more even. Though she still knew Nick better and had more connection with him, I started to feel like she cared about me too.

As far as eating went, Kris and I had our battling moments, but not nearly as many as with mom. We ate a lot outside, so I got away with throwing pieces of the food on the ground out of sight quite a few times. Other than that, I think it was easier for me to eat because it meant we got to go back to our activities.

BROTHER TO THE RESCUE

Mom was continually adding rules to her list and finding new ways to control my eating experiences. The longer the lists got and the more controlled I was, I felt more and more desperate to escape. I was going to need to get more creative and strategic if I was going to outsmart my mom. She might be persistent and watchful, but I was resourceful. This eating disorder started turning my problem-solving skills into overdrive.

I needed to think, how could I get a moment where I knew no one was watching me? It didn't take long before it hit me. It seemed so obvious; I was a little embarrassed I hadn't thought of it sooner.

The bathroom.

I could excuse myself to use the bathroom, lock the door, and have the small moment alone I needed. So, at the next meal, I decided to try it out. I took a big bite of my food — big enough that I had a good amount of food I didn't want to eat in my mouth, but not so much that I couldn't say "I need to go to the bathroom" — and excused myself. I was careful not to walk too fast to the bathroom so I didn't look suspicious and I locked the door behind me. Holy cow, it worked!

I turned my face toward the toilet. This felt a little strange, but it was better than having to eat the food. I didn't want to make any splashing noises in the toilet, so I spit the big chunk of food into my hand and gently lowered it down. I had to be sure I was in the bathroom long enough so it seemed like I had actually gone to the bathroom. I stood silently and waited for a minute to pass. After I felt like the minute was over, I flushed and washed my hands, making sure to take a look back into the toilet bowl to ensure everything had been ejected and my parents could never find the proof.

I was ecstatic; this was genius.

I started implementing my flushing routine into most meals, but I was still careful to not draw attention to my sneaky ways. I could only allow myself to do this once per meal or it might draw my mom's attention. And I would make sure to wait to do it for the foods I really did not want to eat, like a big chunk of chewy pork steak or an accumulated pile of grape skins I collected in my cheeks after eating the soft inside part of the grapes. And it worked for a while. I was flushing food left and right. I was starting to take control.

But I let myself get too comfortable. My mom started to get suspicious when I was excusing myself practically every dinner time. And there was one consequence I hadn't considered in my plotting. So, one time when I got up to head to the bathroom, she intervened.

"I'm coming with you."

"What? I'm just going to the bathroom."

"You can leave the door open."

"You're not going to watch me go to the bathroom."

"I'm sorry, I have to. I know you've been getting rid of food that way."

"No, I haven't!"

"Well, I am going to watch you anyway." She walked with me to the bathroom and put her hand on the door so I couldn't close it. Now what was I going to do? I walked over to the toilet, pulled down my pants, and sat down. Mom stood in the doorway, watching me as I forced myself to pee. I still had a big wad of food stuffed in my cheeks. This was beyond awkward; it was humiliating. I couldn't believe I had slipped up and made my trickery too obvious. And now, for the foreseeable future I would have to expose my body to my parents even if I did really just have to pee. If my mom wasn't there, my dad would have to step in. That was even worse. So that plan turned into a failure. But I wouldn't be defeated. My next move would just have to be smarter.

What else would be unsuspecting? How else could I get rid of food without my mom knowing?

The problem was that mom was too vigilant during mealtimes. But what if I could get rid of the food after the fact? This might work. I couldn't escape to the bathroom anymore, but what if I could make a brief exit to my room?

This time I made sure to plan all of the pieces so mom wouldn't find out. I would leave something in my room so I could say "I need to go grab this," and get away from her watchful eyes. It wouldn't give me a ton of time, but it would be just enough for what I needed to do. I could prance back to my room, quickly spit out my food and stick it under my bed or in a dresser drawer, grab the item I had said I needed and return to the table, being careful to look like I was chewing on my way back. Then, later that night (sometime after everyone was in bed), when no one was thinking about food or what I was doing, I could make my way to the bathroom to flush the food or throw it away.

The first few times I did this, when I returned later, it had become dried out and gross so I didn't really want to touch it. Sometimes, if I forgot it was there for a few days, when I eventually remembered and went to throw it away, I would find mold growing all over it. I decided to start wrapping the food in a few tissues and hiding it so I wouldn't have to look at it when I returned.

My food hiding plan was working flawlessly. Mom never confronted me about leaving (I was careful to be more sporadic this time instead of making it a pattern) and she never searched for any thrown away food.

That's when I got another idea: tissues.

I was starting to get good at this; so good that maybe I could trick my mom in plain sight. If I got up to "blow my nose," but instead put my wad of food in the tissue and threw it away, I just might be able to pull off my flushing trick without needing to go to the bathroom.

Sure enough, it worked. I got up from the table, grabbed a tissue and turned away from my family, made sounds like I was blowing my nose while silently wrapping the tissue around my food, and casually threw it in the trash without a moment's pause from anyone. I was fooling them right in front of their own eyes. Genius.

I was starting to get a good repertoire of tricks up my sleeve, but it still wasn't enough. I needed to get rid of more food. But I was running out of ideas for things I could do by myself. I needed an ally and I knew just who could help me. Nick.

Nick is my brother and just 14 months older than me. Because we are so close in age, we also have a very close relationship. As young kids we would play make believe together with our toys, watch movies and create adventures outside on our farm. As we got older, we joined a lot of the same clubs in school and got to know each other's friends.

Our relationship was especially unique because my brother was diagnosed with Asperger's Syndrome when he was very young, which led him to have struggles that most kids didn't have. This meant I felt like I had to protect him from all of the people who would try to bully him through the years. He had a lot of protective feelings over me too, like any big brother would have for their sister. He was there to comfort me when I was down, give me advice when I was a little off track, and he even saved my life while risking his own during a snowmobile accident one day. Everything we experienced in our childhood, we experienced together and we loved it that way. We relied on each other, trusted each other, and we would do anything for each other. That's why I knew I could convince him to be on my side.

The idea came to me in a moment of struggle during dinner one night. My mom had sliced up an apple for me to eat (along with several other food groups), and after two slices I couldn't take it anymore. There was no way I could finish eating them and I knew putting up a fight with my mom would blow up into a huge event. I couldn't handle that tonight. Everyone else had finished eating already — Dad went back outside to work in the garage, Nick was sitting behind me on the recliner playing his Nintendo and my mom had gone to do something, I wasn't sure what. I saw my opportunity.

"Nick," I whispered. He was very focused on his game. "Nick," I whispered a little louder.

"What?" He looked up to me from his game.

"Can you eat some of my apple slices?" I figured it wasn't too much to ask, he loved apples. I grabbed two slices and held them out toward him.

"I don't really think I should do that… You're supposed to be eating everything." The way he looked at me made me feel bad for asking him. It was a look of sympathy, but also one of a rule follower. He knew about my eating disorder and had watched mom fight with me about finishing food. He knew it was best for me to eat it all, but I could tell there was also a part of him that wanted to take the pain from his little sister. I knew asking was putting him in a tough and uncomfortable situation but I needed help. I was desperate.

"It's just two slices. It won't make that much of a difference for me to not eat them."

"If it won't make that much of a difference, why don't you just eat them?" He's always been so logical. At this moment I did not need logic, I needed the apple slices gone.

"I just don't want to. Please will you eat them?" He looked up hesitantly at my pleading, sad eyes.

"Ugh, fine. But that's all I'm eating." He took the slices and quickly threw them in his mouth. I could tell he wasn't happy with me, but I was relieved. He was the best. He finished the first slice and popped the second in his mouth just in time before my mom reappeared from the bedroom. He acted like nothing had happened, thank goodness, and I took the last bites left on my plate, satisfying my mom for the night.

I hoped Nick wouldn't be mad at me. I didn't mean to use him. I just felt like I had to. But seeing the look on his face as he did my dirty deed made me realize he might not be a reliable technique for me to use to get rid of my food. I knew he wouldn't keep breaking the rules for me. And I didn't want to make him hate me. So, I vowed I'd only do it again if I *really* needed to. For now, I'd have to rely on my hiding skills for some relief.

* * * * *

I realized that maybe I could use these problem-solving and hiding skills in another area of my battle. I learned from the "blowing my nose" trick that the best solution is to hide things in plain sight, but maybe that didn't always have to mean hiding food. One of my biggest problems with this whole thing was the doctors telling my mom that something was wrong with me, that I was underweight and not making enough progress. But what if I did make more progress? Then would they finally let this all end?

All I would have to do is make it look like I was gaining weight, even if I wasn't. And I knew just how to do it. Whenever they weighed me and did routine tests at my appointments, they asked me to take off my clothes and put on a gown. But they didn't make me take off my underwear or socks. It wasn't much to work with, but it would have to do. Anything with my underwear was out because part of the routine was the doctor feeling up my abdomen and groin area. But my socks were fair game. I would just need to find something relatively heavy that would tip the scale a bit, but that would not make my feet stand out if shoved in my socks.

The first thought that came to my head was metal washers. My inspiration came from going along to help my dad with numerous small jobs and hearing about his construction work. I knew he had plenty of washers laying around in our garage and shop. They were small and flat enough that they wouldn't be easily seen, but they could add a bit of weight if I chose the right ones. I'd just have to wrap them in something soft and step lightly so they didn't clank when I stepped on the scale.

I found a couple washers that had a diameter about as wide as the bottom of my foot and decided to wrap them in tissues (my new best friends, it was turning out). I tested them by putting them in my sock and walking around my bedroom. I tried to think through what might happen at my next appointment, but I just couldn't think of anything going wrong. Hopefully, this would give me the weight I needed; subtle enough to not seem suspicious, but large enough that we could ease up on all eating regimens and life changes.

The next day came and I was ready to execute my plan. My mom was grabbing her purse and papers to write down any notes, while I quickly shoved my wrapped-up washers into my socks. We got in the car and headed out on the 90-minute drive down to the Cities. I could feel my heart beating with nerves about this new plan, but I just had to calm down and be confident. I couldn't let on that anything was different about today. Tucked inside my shoes, my toes couldn't help but to anxiously curl around the small weights and their shabby wrapping.

As we made our way through the lobby, up the stairs, and into the doctor's exam room, every step felt heavier and more awkward, the rings of the washers pressing an indent into the bottom of my foot that kept reminding me of their presence. I was starting to doubt this plan; surely my mom or the doctor would be able to feel the pressure illuminating from the washers in my sock just as I could and would call me out. But I had to follow through now — we were already here.

I carefully undressed, being sure not to ruffle my socks in the process. With only a gown around me, my trickery felt even more exposed. But my facial expression stayed confident as the nurse made her way in. First, she took my height, then it was time to step on the scale. I placed the left foot on as light as a feather, and gently the right foot followed. To my excitement, there was no noise from the washers. I looked over to the nurse as she checked the screen for my weight. I thought I could see a slight smile as she looked from the screen to her papers to write down the result.

Holy cow, what if this was working?

I sat back on the patient bed to wait for the doctor to come in to finish her tests and share her thoughts. When she finally arrived, she went through all the other checks, and I just prayed my mom couldn't see the little bundles at the bottom of my feet. I tried to tip my toes down in an effort to conceal what I could. Finally, the doctor made her way to her rolling stool to look over everything on the paperwork. Now time for the fruits of my labor.

"It looks like there's been some decent progress," she smiled at both me and my mom. "Keep up the good work, and we'll see you again in a few days, if there aren't any questions."

Excuse me, what?

That was supposed to be the part where she said I'm free to leave and never come back. If I had done such "good work," why weren't we done? What made me the maddest was that they didn't even know about the weights in my socks. What if I had actually done more of the hard work to gain weight? It wouldn't have even mattered. She still would've given me some baby-worthy compliment and asked me back for the next round. I was pissed. And hopelessness was starting to set in. Nothing I was going to do would ever make enough difference to get me out of here, to make this end.

When I got home, I threw the washers into my dresser drawer still wrapped in the tissues. For all the anxiety it took to make that stunt happen, it was not worth the end result. If no weight change was going to make this end, I would just have to keep getting rid of food for me to win. It was the only way.

Mom's Perspective:

I had to be so vigilant, paying attention to every move Alexa made when there was food involved. So, it wasn't just a matter of me sitting with her until she finished, it was a constant game of wits. Damn, the eating disorder is a ferocious little sucker, and this is exactly what I was up against. This was about winning. It was a battle I did not sign up for, but took all the punches for.

I remember when I caught the bathroom tactic. Alexa was going too often and at weird times for it to be a real bathroom visit. I could not stop her from using the bathroom — that would be cruel. All I could do was make her go before eating and then watch her immediately following to make sure we were in the clear and the food had gone down. I hated having to stand and hold the door. It might have felt like an invasion, but that is what the eating disorder wanted me to feel. Tactics like this were the reason I had to put so many rules in place.

There might have been moments of genius in the eating disorder's eyes, but I caught on to most of it (at least that is what I thought).

Withering

DARK DESPAIR

An eating disorder has the chance of destroying everything in its path. I was a near fatal victim myself.

Aside from our home life and everything needed there, I had a lot going on in my work life at the time as well. My full-time job was especially hectic that year because I was organizing two national events. On top of these, I was also in charge of a regular schedule of educational events for three states. One major annual meeting alone is the work of one individual and I had four other major events to plan and organize.

Somewhere in there, I also put together a 10-year review of our foundation's activities. It included projects we completed or funded and a full 10-year budget review. I was responsible for nearly all the paperwork needed in the binder we provided our board of directors that year. I was involved in many projects and in most of our state agency partnerships.

A few months earlier, Nick had to undergo GI surgery for a stomach issue he had been battling over the winter. It turned out that he had some anxiety issues as well, so we were also receiving some counseling for him. Early in Nick's diagnosis, I decided there would be no drugs unless they were absolutely called for. This was one of those times when drugs were offered and I declined. But that decision meant more attention for Nick was required on my part. I was already stretched, but I stuck to my decision.

I mostly worked from home, so I did have the flexibility to deal with things throughout the day as I saw fit. Regarding work, I just had to get the jobs done — it didn't matter what time of day I did them. I did have to travel during that time, but I had been traveling for my job since I started in 2003. In fact, one year I counted over 200 days of travel. On occasion, when the boss was in town, I would work at our main office in New Ulm, Minnesota which is about 45 minutes south of home.

I believe it was early July when one of these days arrived and I was headed to the office.

Frustration had been building with the counselors for Alexa because I didn't feel like they were getting to her underlying problem. I wasn't getting much help, if any, from Robert with either Alexa or Nick. In reviewing my journal, I realized he was regularly saying things that the counselor said we shouldn't, like "just eat." These became part of the problem too and I started seeing him as an adversary rather than a partner. The only saving grace was that I had Kris on my team.

There were multiple occasions where I wrote in my journal how exhausted I was. I even wrote down a time when Robert took off for an evening bike ride and I noted that I hadn't exercised in about four months. Every part of me was running low; mentally, physically, emotionally and even spiritually.

That morning, Alexa was having a rough time. I simply reminded her what needed to be done and left it at that. An eating disorder wants constant negotiation and I wasn't going to engage. I had to go to my basement office to get ready for work in New Ulm and pack some things up for the day. I was barely out of the room when Robert started trying to engage with Alexa.

I heard him say "get eating" and "get a better attitude." That really pissed me off. Not only was that escalating the situation, but it took me right back to high school when my dad told me to put a smile on my face or he'd take away my exchange program.

Alexa finished eating in the required time — barely — and I had everything ready to go when Kris arrived. I could finally get on the road to New Ulm.

I was driving with the music on but still ruminating about what had happened and the extra work I had to do to counteract Robert. I started crying, wondering how I would ever survive this.

About 15 minutes into my drive is a set of railroad tracks. As I stopped, I laid my head on the steering wheel in utter despair, tears rolling down my face. I remember looking to the left of the tracks, seeing a cemetery and *thinking of all the struggle going on around me. I remember thinking "what is the common denominator here?"*

Me. Work was a struggle, Nick's anxiety, Alexa's eating disorder — I am the common denominator. Perhaps it would be best if I were gone.

There was no train. Just me and the tracks. I eased a few feet forward but not fully across the tracks. The tears kept flowing as I hunched down on the steering wheel. Just moments after I started my despair loop, a voice inside said, "if not you, then who?"

I took a giant gasp of breath and noticed what I had just been thinking. I felt a moment of gratitude for the save and a short pouring of new energy entered my body. Yes. Robert wasn't going to do it, my family wasn't going to do it and it wasn't Kris's responsibility — it had to be me.

The rest of the day was kind of a blur. I was numb, but survived. I masked up for my boss and coworkers. Kris had the kids until 4pm and they'd be okay until I got home around 5pm. Supper was another hour to completion but nothing I wasn't already used to. The last thing I wrote in my journal that day was "my exhaustion is taking its toll."

God breathed a little life back into me — and perhaps strengthened my resolve for the work ahead. I simply had to navigate it day by day, praying for extra strength each night before bed. Thankfully, this strength was granted each time.

There really are no words to describe what happened. It really was the core of my being standing firm — holding myself solid in the job that needed to be done at the time — to help Alexa heal.

Every time I think about that moment, I am in tears all over again. My body feels every sensation of a heavy heart, barely able to breathe, near guttural emptiness. It is most literally the lowest point in my life, and I have experienced a lot of low points. This was the one and only time I have considered my own disappearance. What was underneath was overwhelm (who can be prepared for this?), fear (not knowing what would happen), and loneliness (little support).

It makes me a little depressed, looking back, because there were plenty of people around me who should have seen my condition and asked how they could help. I was in such a state of low there was no way for me to ask — I barely knew what I was doing. The facility meant to heal, sadly, did not provide the support I needed to navigate this disease as a parent. I wish it was more understood that treating eating disorders needs to include support for family members.

TIME TO QUIT

I can't do this. Something must go. I simply cannot be a good mom, save my daughter and work crazy hours at my job. I had pretty much checked out as a wife.

About mid-summer, I finally talked myself into the need to let something go. If I tried to keep up this pace, more than one of us might not survive. I realized I had to talk to my boss about quitting. I couldn't bring my whole self to work and my priority was my kids.

After the internal decision was made, I had to approach Robert. I recall him being outside because that's where he was all summer. I found him and told him I couldn't keep up and needed help. I suggested that he go back to work. The company he used to work for had great pay and amazing benefits so I could leave my job which, at the time, carried our family health insurance. He had left the company a few years earlier, after I started working full-time at my organization. He enjoyed farming more and, when the opportunity arose, we had agreed that I could cover the insurance and he could quit. He was working 12-hour shifts, alternating days and nights, which can wreak havoc on the body.

I knew it would be a stretch. I understood why he might not want to go back — but this wasn't about him, it was about our family. And I didn't see any other way.

He wasn't doing the work of parenting, so I needed to be able to focus more of my time on it. I remember the exact phrase he spoke when I asked him to go back to work.

"Why would I do that?"

I was taken aback.

I expected a bunch of reasons for not going back, or maybe even some other alternatives. But I didn't expect a straight out 'why the heck would I do that?'

I'm certain I said something equally hostile back — probably that I wasn't surprised. He hadn't stepped up so far.

That response became another validation that I/we were not going to receive any kind of support. He said just to have faith that it would work out. While I believe faith is a big part, I also believe you must act. Faith doesn't give you the right to shirk responsibility. That's how I felt about it. So, yet again, I wasn't going to get any help.

I was thinking, Really? You don't care about your family? I said I was not comfortable going without insurance. This could get ridiculously expensive and, even then, we don't know if it will work. I had no idea how long this was going to take or what else we might have to add for treatments. I worked too darn hard to lose everything to this. I was angry, disappointed, disgusted, and feeling deeply vulnerable and abandoned.

Either way, I had to talk to my boss. I remember having a lot of angst about the conversation. I didn't want to quit. I worked hard to get to where I was. I didn't want to give it up. I was working from home with decent pay in a small rural town. When would I ever get another opportunity like that? I did not want to go back to long drives to a workplace. Plus, it's hard enough for women in conservation careers and only more so if they take an extended period off. People wonder about how committed you are.

Why is it that women always must make these kinds of sacrifices?

Even if others didn't appreciate how hard it was, I did like the career I was building.

This internal exchange was brutal. In the end, however, I concluded that I just couldn't give the job the proper attention and had to shift that attention to my kids.

I mustered up the courage to speak to my boss on the phone. I know I couldn't have had that same conversation in person. He already knew about Alexa's diagnosis because I had to shift my work hours to accommodate doctor's appointments. On those days, I often started earlier or worked later. I told him I was exhausted and that I couldn't perform anywhere near what was expected of me. I expressed that it wasn't fair to my coworkers or the organizations who relied on my work. I simply couldn't meet expectations.

My boss understood what was going on, expressed compassion, and told me to wait. He would see what he could figure out. We quickly ran through some major projects and decided what could wait.

I felt good that I had stood up for what needed to be done and there was a sense of relief that he didn't immediately accept my pseudo-resignation.

It wasn't too many days later when he called back. He said that the board had agreed they would keep me on full-time with full pay and benefits. I should just do what I could. He had our executive assistant reach out to ask how she could help. I also received some extra assistance in some of the educational events I was in charge of. That took a great deal of pressure off, at least in the short term. I thanked him for his support and confidence.

There was no timeline at that moment, and we would check in again after a few months. I was relieved beyond measure. At least one giant weight had been lifted from my shoulders in the form of health insurance. I also didn't have to feel guilty for not giving the usual 150% (most staff did the job of at least 2 people). I still probably did the normal work of one person. I was just more able to drop the guilt of not giving it my all — in other words, to the extent I had before.

I often wonder if the board was actually involved in that decision or not. Those kinds of decisions didn't normally go to the board. I never asked and, at that time, I didn't care. Something else was possible. I could keep insurance and pay more attention to the needs of my kids. That was such an incredible gift and relief. I informed Robert of the decision that night and we didn't talk about it again.

I was starting some critical projects at that time that are still important milestones today. I like to think my boss felt they couldn't afford not to have me there in whatever capacity I was able to provide. That's what I tell myself anyway.

In those next days, I didn't rush quite as quickly to work. I allowed myself some extra coffee time in the sunroom to decompress after breakfast.

Occasionally, I took a ride on my bike. I know I didn't let go of as many work items as I could have — the mistaken belief that I am irreplaceable, that no one can do it like me. I can also admit that, working in a male-dominated field, I felt I needed to do more to prove myself. Regardless, I felt some relief from the shift.

CISCO

The fight against food and my mom was relentless. Of course, there were days where everyone was watching too closely so I couldn't sneak food away, or I had already snuck some and couldn't do any more for fear of being caught (I really couldn't afford to screw up the only master plan of mine that was still working). On those days, right before I reached my breaking point, there was one thing to soothe my distress: Cisco.

"Alexa, go sit outside with Cisco for 5 minutes, then come back in and finish eating." My mom knew he was my saving grace, so in those roughest moments, she sent me out for a quick break. I would open the front porch door, and there he would be. Forty-five pounds of pure love in the form of a dog.

Cisco, an Australian shepherd/border collie cross, was my best friend. We found him and his siblings online the year prior, and when we went to meet them, we knew instantly he was the one. A calm, sweet ball of gray fur splotched with black spots. He had white socks around his paws and the classic white border collie band from his nose all the way behind his ears and around his neck. His nose was speckled black and pink, he had one eye that was brown and one eye that was mostly blue and about one quarter brown, and I thought he was the most beautiful puppy I had ever seen. Not to mention his personality was a perfect mix of laid back and playful. It seemed as though we both had an immediate understanding that we would become best friends. His first night home, he didn't even cry as puppies often do. He slept through the night and was ready to spend our first full day by each other's side.

I had taken some dog training classes prior to adding Cisco to the family and I was excited to do it all on my own with this new puppy. Watching Cisco quickly pick up new commands and get excited to work together only continued to grow our bond, along with endless amounts of playing and snuggles. I also had the goal of trying something new with Cisco: dog agility. My mom signed us up for some beginner's classes and soon we were navigating courses of jumps, tunnels, teeter totters and more. Being with Cisco was my new passion; he was my best friend.

When things got tough during my eating disorder, Cisco was the only one that I knew for sure was not judging me and would give me love no matter what. Luckily, our kitchen was set up in such a way that even though Cisco was an outside dog, I could still access him pretty easily during mealtimes. In our kitchen, I always sat on the furthest right chair on the island. To my right was the wide opening of an entryway from our porch that had a giant glass window overlooking our porch, front yard, and driveway. It was as if Cisco could sense from outside whether I needed him or not, because whenever I needed reassurance, his handsome, sweet eyes would be peeking through the right bottom corner of the window.

I always felt if he could speak, he would surely be saying "I want to be in there with you to comfort you, but if you need me, I'll be right out here." Sometimes seeing his face was enough, and after about a minute Cisco would lay down beneath the window to take a nap in the sun. But other times, I took his gaze as the sign I needed more. As I approached the door, his short stub of a tail would wag like crazy. I would walk outside to be greeted by hand kisses and leg rubs. I sat down next to him on the stairs and he followed suit, lowering his energy accordingly after sensing I needed comfort. As my fingers ran through his soft fur, I could instantly feel pressure fall from my shoulders. It felt to me that, if I closed my eyes, I could bury myself in his fur and escape for just a few moments. I could tell him anything, I could cry with him, I could just sit in silence and pet him, we could play or train to bring the mood up. No matter what I needed, Cisco was ready. Of course, he got what he wanted too; pets, treats, or play time.

I could talk on and on about Cisco and sometimes, in therapy appointments, I did. When I walked into my first therapist's room, I of course noticed the squishy objects lining the windowsill, the abstract pictures on the wall and books lining a shelf (your common therapist aesthetic

I suppose). But what I noticed that most others probably didn't was a small rectangular box attached to the ceiling. On it were blue sticker letters that spelled "Cisco" with some lines above it. I knew it was the technology company's name and logo, but it was a happy reminder of my best friend even while I was away from home. It didn't take my therapist long to notice my occasional glances at the ceiling. "I notice you looking up at something. What are you looking at?"

"My dog's name is Cisco, just like that box on the ceiling," I told her as I pointed to it without averting my eyes from it.

"Oh, ok. Do you want to tell me about him?"

"Sure." I filled her in on what he looked like, our adventures, anything I could to keep the conversation on Cisco and not on eating or anything else eating disorder related.

She jotted down some notes during our conversation, so it was no surprise that the next therapy session started off referencing Cisco.

"Last week you told me that box," she pointed up the ceiling, "reminds you of your dog. And you told me he helps you a lot when you're struggling with food at home. What do you do when you're struggling at school? Or out in public?"

I shrugged my shoulders, not really wanting to address her questions about struggling with food.

"Well, I was thinking, your dog can't go everywhere with you, right?" I nodded.

"But you said petting his fur sometimes makes you feel good?" I nodded again, not sure where she was going with this.

"Maybe you can try this." She held out her hand to me, in it a rectangular white brush about the size of a match box. "It's soft, like his fur. You can carry it in your pocket or in a bag with you, and whenever you're feeling stressed or upset you can feel it to remind you of Cisco."

I could hardly process fast enough what just happened. I nodded in agreement to satisfy her, but I was baffled. On what earth is a brush the same as a dog? Sure, it was soft and felt nice, but it wasn't Cisco. Cisco was a living being, there was more to his comforting effect than just stroking his fur.

I suddenly wished I hadn't told her anything about Cisco. My feelings of not being understood came rushing back, but on a whole different level. Not only did she not understand me, she didn't understand Cisco either (or our relationship) and had decided to use my story about him to her advantage, as a tool.

It felt like there was nothing I could safely tell her anymore. Our sessions soon became a routine of surface level questions from her and nods or small generic responses from me. But this wouldn't be the last time Cisco was used as a mechanism against my eating disorder. And the next time it would be much worse.

* * * * *

It started out like any other meal in the thick of my eating disorder. Food was put on my plate. A timer was set to tick down from 45 minutes. All there was to do was finish everything within the designated time. If only it were that easy. To people who don't struggle with food, 45 minutes might seem like more than enough time to eat a meal but, to me, this felt like a nearly impossible task. I tried to give it my best effort as I started out, but when the timer was half done, I had barely made a dent on my plate. Hopelessness set in, and quickly shifted to active, aggressive avoidance. There was no point in trying to finish eating when there was no way it could be finished in that amount of time and mom would get mad at me anyway.

It didn't take long for mom to notice me sitting there, staring into the void, not touching my food for minutes on end. "You better keep eating, Alexa. There's only 20 minutes left on the timer."

"I know," I said matter-of-factly without making eye contact with her or moving from my position with my knees curled up against the counter. She made an extra loud sigh and turned to face the stove, obviously trying to brainstorm how to fix this situation because she could tell I was not about to budge. It had already been a difficult day for meals; earlier in the day I had also struggled, and nothing seemed to be helping me eat more or faster. As a result, mom was becoming less patient and I was becoming stronger in my resistance.

"How about I add a few minutes to the timer? Will that help?" I shrugged my shoulders in response. She walked over to adjust to the timer on our stove, and I put another small bite in my mouth. When she noticed I started eating, she went back to the bedroom for who-knows-what.

But as the clock kept ticking down, I could see this was still a pointless effort, so I stopped eating yet again. The clock was down to ten minutes left. My mom re-entered the room, took one look at my plate and groaned out loud.

"Alexa, you need to eat the food!"

"I can't!"

"Alexa, there are ten minutes left on the timer. If you are not done eating by the time it is done, we are getting rid of Cisco." My eyes opened wide in shock. She couldn't be serious.

"You can't; he's my dog."

"I can, Alexa. And I will unless you finish eating."

My heart felt like it fell out of my body at that moment. There were so many reasons this wasn't right. Cisco was my dog — I paid for him and I took care of him. Plus, we both needed each other. Images popped into my head of someone else having him and treating him wrong, or worse, killing him. He didn't deserve this at all. Not to mention he was the only thing these days that actually made me happy.

And mom wanted to make that disappear?

I felt like I had no control. If she tried to take him away from me, what could I, a ten-year-old, possibly do to stop her? I imagined trying to tackle her down before she could get to Cisco, but I was too small for that to work. I imagined making a dash outside to run away just me and Cisco, but I would need time to gather supplies for us and she would be able to find us if we tried to dart now. I couldn't risk losing my best friend, so the only option was to try to eat as fast as I could.

My body was tense, and I was furious. I started throwing the food from my plate into my mouth and aggressively chewing to make a point to my mom of how ridiculous this was. I was so scared I would choke eating this much food this quickly, but with the clock ticking down I didn't have time to think of another option. The food felt like bricks traveling down my throat. I continued to bang my fork and plate around as I ate to show my mom I could be as outrageous as her. Somehow, miraculously, I managed to eat the food before the timer ran out. My body was utterly exhausted. My mom took my plate and told me I could finally leave the kitchen.

I sulked my way into my bedroom, feeling like I could collapse right into myself. What if I hadn't finished the food? Would she really have taken Cisco away? What would I have done if she did? I felt so scared, lonely and depressed as the only logical answer came to my head. I would have to kill myself.

I could not be happy in this life without Cisco. I would not be able to keep doing this without Cisco. I pictured myself walking into our 4-stall garage, taking Dad's gun down from the wall, and pointing it at myself. The thought of a gun pointing at me was terrifying, but the thought of living without Cisco terrified me more.

That night I curled into bed more defeated than I had ever been, so much so I could not even cry. The fact that my mind could even think that way petrified me. Maybe I had just saved Cisco, but when would someone finally come to save me?

Mom's Perspective:

I regret that I even considered threatening to take away Cisco. Instantaneously after I said it, I felt remorse.

I was deeply relieved when she ate her food on time because I really did not know that I could follow through with my threat. But since I made it, I prepared for the possibility. I figured I could take him to my parent's house about 30 minutes away and keep him there until she could prove she could put in the work. In reality, there was no way to remove him from our home. No one cares for Cisco the way she does. He is one of our story's heroes.

There were many times throughout the eating disorder that I told Alexa to "go pet your dog." He also was part of her recovery in something that she enjoyed doing with training and classes, which took her mind off of eating.

CAGED ANIMAL

At this point, I was pretty dejected. I'd been battling this eating disorder for what seemed like ages with hardly anything positive to show for it. It felt like I was always eating — the time in between meals felt nonexistent. There seemed to be more and more friction building up — between me and food, between me and my mom, between me and myself. Some part of the system was bound to blow.

While summer was a refuge for most people, for me it was looking more like a prison. At school I could get away with more because the staff had other kids to watch too, but over the summer I was singled out. Constantly. Just a few days into the summer, I was already exhausted and all I craved was lenience. A new day was usually a fresh start for me, but this day was different. I was already sad and mad, and I just wanted a break. But while I craved mercy, my mom desired progress and her patience was lacking. Little did she know, I was about to completely lose mine.

Breakfast was the usual: a protein/vitamin chocolate milk and three chocolate chip pancakes. As the syrup soaked in, making the pancakes heavy and dense, I knew I wanted no part of this meal or this day. Likely sensing this, my mom came over to give some "encouraging words." Fuel to my inner burning fire.

"It's not that easy! You don't get it!"

"Alexa, I'm just trying to help you feel better about eating." She took a step back, not in a shocked or scared way, but almost seemed to be adding space to the situation to bring it on. I could see she didn't plan on cutting any slack today; she had already snipped at my dad earlier over what seemed like nothing.

"It's never going to work!" I didn't just mean now. I meant ever. Nothing we did was ever going to work, I knew that now. I was forever broken, and this was my breaking point. I could feel the anger rising from my feet to my head, rising like the mercury in a thermometer. I couldn't help but let the tears escape.

I extended my arms from the countertop, tipping the bar stool so only the back two feet were on the floor. Latching my fingers under the lip of the counter, I pulled my arms back in to send the front of the bar stool slamming back onto the floor. It sent a shock wave through my back and neck up to my head. I kept extending out to balance the chair and quickly crashing it back into the floor. Between the tears and the banging of the chair, my head was hot and throbbing. I was manifesting the inner pain that no one seemed to understand.

"Alexa, you need to stop banging the chair, you're going to break it."

Why was she concerned about a chair breaking when her daughter was breaking right in front of her eyes? If my obvious pain wasn't sending the message, all that was left to do was disappear. I stormed to the bathroom and turned around to slam the door shut. But of course, there my mom stood, her hand holding the door open.

"The door has to stay open, you know that."

How could she be so nonchalant right now? My mind was spinning, not sure where to go or what to do. It felt like my insides were ripping themselves apart. My head was pounding and my fists involuntarily clenched my nails into my palms. My legs were tingling, waiting to provide their share of chaos to the mix. I kicked the door into the bathroom cabinets and ran back into the living room.

In the open space there weren't many places for someone to disappear, even someone as little as me. But I had to hide somewhere; I couldn't take this anymore. I tucked myself behind the couch where there was just enough space between it and the wall. Kneeling there didn't feel like enough. There had to be some way to make my pain evident. To turn my mental pain into physical pain. I wrapped my arms in front of my chest and started scraping into my arms, feeling a release with every new pressure of my nails digging into my skin. Not hard enough to draw blood, but hard enough to leave a mark. It still wasn't enough. My fists clenched back up and I threw my fist sideways into the wall closest to me. Again. And again. And again. It still wasn't enough. I couldn't escape from the torment I was feeling inside.

"I feel like a caged animal!" As I screamed it out, I darted out from behind the couch and headed toward the stairs leading to our basement.

"Let's take a minute and try to calm down. You're out of control." My mom took a step towards me to try to stop my momentum, but there was nothing she could do. In fact, she was the reason I was this way.

"Just stop, you're just a bitch!" My throat was burning from crying and screaming. I paused for a moment in shock that I just swore at mom and she didn't react one bit. Even when it was directed at her. For a moment I felt a bit of power, but even that wasn't enough to ease my pain. As I stood on the steps, pausing to take in the moment, I thought back to my comment — "I feel like a caged animal." It was then that I knew where I needed to go, where I belonged. If I was like an animal locked in a zoo, I was meant to be in a cage.

I ran back up the stairs, through the kitchen and out the door that led to our garage. From there, I reached for the door that led outside. I swung it back and slammed it hard into the frame. And then again, harder. And another time harder. I could feel the walls of the garage shaking and it only added to the pounding in my head. Finally, I exited the garage and walked straight out towards Cisco's kennel. He rounded the corner of the house just as I was reaching for the kennel door. I never thought this kennel was a very good place for Cisco to sleep, but it would be a perfect enclosure for an animal like me.

I latched the kennel shut, leaving Cisco standing outside wondering what was going on, and crawled into the doghouse that was kept inside. There was some straw covering the floor and a few tattered blankets used to keep Cisco warm at night toward the back of the house. Spiders crept their way along the walls to find a crevice to hide in. Usually, I would be disgusted to be inside the doghouse, but today the straw, dirt, spiders, and darkness felt appropriate.

I breathed in the stale air and curled my knees up to my chest. For a long time, I sat still in that position. Like a caged animal in a zoo, a sense of learned helplessness kicked in. This was my new normal. I would forever be under the reign of my mom, throwing food down my throat that I didn't actually want to eat, but nowhere else to go and nothing else to do. Something about this realization calmed my breathing and slowly released me from the trance I was in.

I looked out from my hiding place and brought myself back into reality. Cisco was sitting near the kennel door facing me. Though I didn't think this place was the best for him, I suddenly felt an overwhelming sadness that I had locked him out of what he probably felt was his home. Not to mention he was probably confused as to what I was doing and why he couldn't be with me. I maneuvered my way out of the doghouse, to the kennel door, and opened it for Cisco to come in.

We sat together on the cement, leaning against the wire cage walls. With each stroke of Cisco's fur, my heart rate decreased and the heat running through my veins subsided more and more. I knew I would have to go back inside and face the inevitable. But a few more minutes in this metal prison was heavenly compared to some more time in the prison of the breakfast table.

Mom's Perspective:

The kids were out of school by this time — it was June. They were up for the morning, but Alexa was playing her Nintendo DS on the couch and had not yet made it up to the island table for breakfast. I could see she seemed to be getting frustrated with her game.

Robert asked her to go get breakfast and she paid no attention. She just kept playing her game and did not make a move. I waited somewhat impatiently to see if Robert would follow-through on his request. Hearing nothing, I told her to come over for breakfast and turn the game off. She was in a bad mood. I tried to say something positive (I wrote that in my journal but didn't note what) and then all hell broke loose. I could see that her eyes had gone cold and distant — almost evil. It was scary. My baby was definitely not present in this body in front of me.

As you read, you will notice my recollection differs from Alexa's. We have each shared what we remember and made an agreement not to alter each other's experiences in this writing.

The way I remember it, she marched outside and sat next to the dog-house for a while. I just let her be because I figured Cisco would come over and there wasn't much she could hurt herself with. After a short time — maybe 10 minutes, she came in through the garage, slamming the door. She shoved me out of the way and called me "bitch" a few times on the way to the bathroom. She tried locking herself in, but I grabbed the door handle before she could get it locked and held the door open. I asked Nick to grab the phone for me and I dialed the doctor's office to see if I could reach Dr. X. I knew there was nothing I could say to her that would matter in this moment, good or bad. She was out of control and I couldn't think of anything else to do. I needed help. As I was on hold, Alexa came out of the bathroom and immediately tried to hide behind the couch.

Dr. X was not in and, by the time I got off the phone, she had settled down a little bit. I could see a small sparkle in her eye that indicated she was arriving back with us. She finally came up to the breakfast table and calmed down enough to say she was ready to talk. It was then she said she felt like she was a caged animal. I asked her if she understood that you don't get in the cage with that kind of animal and she nodded in agreement. I told her that was a great way to describe how she was feeling. Inside, I was amazed that she could verbalize feeling like that, considering the extreme state she had been in.

I gave her a hug and granted her a little extra leniency that morning. It took her about an hour and a half to finish breakfast, but I didn't say anything about it. She went to her room and got dressed for the day. Shortly after, Kris arrived to pick her and Nick up to go to the pool.

I briefly explained to Kris what had happened because Alexa had just recently finished breakfast and they were already near lunch time. I told her I hoped that the episode would be all for the day, but also wanted to prepare her for the worst. I knew she could handle whatever might come up.

As soon as they left, I went to sit in the sunroom and recoup a bit before heading to work in my basement office. I was already mentally drained and it was only 10am.

When I think about the evilness in her eyes that day, it scares me. Thankfully, I never saw those cold, dark and blank eyes ever again and I am so grateful. What is impressive to me is how she could connect to her own internal dialogue right after the incident. I believe that is what makes her so wise today. She can see behind people's masks, including mine. And that is a great gift.

Pruning

GALAPAGOS RESET

Sometimes a little change in location and leaving behind all your struggles is the best way to reset. That's what I felt like the Galapagos Islands did for us.

In 2009, about 6 months before Alexa's diagnosis, I had put a few thousand dollars down as a deposit on a trip to the Galapagos Islands, which included my Mom and Alexa. The trip was in the works for about four years prior with a friend and colleague.

We had been sitting at dinner at our annual trade show and the question came up: if you could go anywhere in the world, where would it be?

"That's easy," I said. "The Galapagos." My friend, who was sitting directly across from me on a table of 20 people said "No way, me too. Let's go!"

We agreed we'd need a few years to save. She did all the planning and found a great tour company that was very environmentally conscious. All the rest of us had to do was pay and show up. I was used to doing all the planning for trips, so this was especially exciting for me.

Because Robert did not want to go, I asked my Mom and then ended up having Alexa join us too. She would be celebrating her birthday during the trip, which added a special touch. When we initially got the diagnosis and started the emotional journey, I wasn't thinking about the trip. But when final payment was due a few months prior to the trip, I had a lot of soul searching to do. Of course, losing my investment in the trip played a role, as did the years of dreaming and planning for it.

If we go, how will I handle food? How will we even know what food is available? Will this send the wrong message — that you can still be rewarded for "bad" behavior? I went back and forth for a couple of weeks. I finally concluded that maybe we both just needed a major break from where we were. My Mom would be along to be back up if needed and a companion when I got too stressed.

Luckily, we spent a little time in Quito before heading to the islands and got to see that chicken was readily available. There was always plenty of fruit, bread, and desserts. I also decided I didn't care if she ate chicken and ice cream all day, every day as long as she got the calories in. It turns out she did eat a lot of chicken and ice cream, but we also had fruit — so fresh I've never tasted anything like it. Plus, I brought along some peanut butter, crackers, and granola bars so we always had that along if we needed familiar food. We actually came back with a lot of those same snacks because we didn't need them.

After we landed on the island, we took a short boat ride from the airport to our first hotel. That short ride gave us a glimpse of the spectacular beauty ahead of us — schools of colorful fish in clear blue water. We also ended up in the highest room at the hotel with walls of glass, giving us the most incredible view of the area.

My initial calm turned to stress with our first excursion. We came back to the boat and, as we boarded, the guides pointed in the direction we'd be traveling. I could see the waves, 10 feet and higher. Alexa was nervous and I worried this would lead to an upset stomach, further complicating our situation. I decided she should lay her head on my lap and close her eyes for the short ride. She didn't resist that suggestion at all.

Thankfully, going through the large waves took less than 10 minutes. When we landed in a little cove, it didn't take long for our spirits to soar again. The island was covered with lizards, beautiful fine sand and hundreds of birds flying around, all different species. We were immediately taken in by the beauty around us, leaving the eating disorder and our nerves quickly behind.

We soon learned we would be doing rocky boat rides in 2-hour increments as we headed to each new island — five in total. On the first long ride, we attempted to sing "99 bottles of beer on the wall" in Spanish. I think we made it to about 80 before our tough-girl attitudes turned into stomach tossing surrender.

After that, we all took Dramamine, laid back and closed our eyes. As Alexa laid on my lap, I attempted to ease the blows of each wave with my body. Those were long rides but, because we sensed what awaited upon landing, taking the Dramamine wasn't a hard choice for any of us to make. In hindsight, our first clue about taking Dramamine should have been when the guides, local islanders, took it for themselves on the first long ride.

One of the best days was Alexa's birthday. We rode out to a cove to snorkel with sea lions in clear, shallow water. Then, we headed to Kicker Rock, where the water was much deeper and darker. She got in the water close to the boat for a few minutes then decided not to get out further. I look at the picture from that short time in the water and see a smile with a little nervousness underneath. I don't blame her — you couldn't see very deep and, while the season was early, there was a possibility of seeing hammerhead sharks. I was quite uneasy myself.

Alexa decided to stay with my Mom on the boat as the rest of us snorkeled around the rock with the boat following us. I don't know what my Mom and Alexa did while we were snorkeling; I was just happy to come back to the boat and see a smiling little girl.

On the way back to shore, the captain asked if Alexa wanted to drive and of course, she said yes. We thought she'd just be up for a few polite minutes, but then the driver directed her to head toward an island in the distance and proceeded to go below. I think she drove for an hour with her shoulders proudly held high. I watched every moment. I glimpsed my little girl again.

That evening, I had called ahead for a cake after dinner — cake is our birthday tradition. We sang happy birthday as they brought it out. When we were done singing a man came over to ask if that was my daughter. It turned out that his daughter was having her 11th birthday too — they were from Canada. We shared a few stories and took some pictures of our families together. I love that the girls still keep in touch, on occasion, more than 10 years later.

The guides were also incredible. I recall one day when Alexa was just growly. One of the young men noticed and started distracting her with curiosity questions and pointing to some cool animals and rock formations. She latched onto the guide and didn't leave his side most of the day, a smile back on her face.

About three quarters of the way through the trip, we were on a long hike to the Sierra Negra volcano. There is a point along the hike where people can stop and rest if they don't want to go any farther. Being the adventurer, I wanted to keep going. My Mom and Alexa wanted to stay behind. I was a little nervous, but the trip had been going so well, I thought if we were gone for 30 minutes or so, everyone would be fine. It was a warm enough day and we had plenty of supplies along.

When our small group got to the peak of the volcano, it was actually a very rare, amazingly clear day and we could see several other islands from that point. The guide asked if we could stay a while longer to enjoy the rare view. I think we ended up being gone for 3 or 4 hours. I fully suspected my Mom and Alexa would have scowls on their faces when we returned. Instead, Alexa ran over to show me some cool pictures of a Galapagos Hawk that was hanging out with them that day. I was so relieved and enjoyed hearing the stories from their sit spot.

A couple of things that happened on this trip helped, I think. First, we dropped the struggle a bit — she could eat whatever, as long as she ate enough. Second, the scenery and such huge diversity of animals kept us in awe and wonder and a lot less thinking about the struggle. Third, we got a little time with each other, sharing fun times without the stress of anyone else. Finally, we were with a group of strong, amazing, and fun women — all biologists. She got to experience other women who showed her how vast her future could be.

I asked two of them to share their perspectives on our family dynamic during the trip and they just described us as being present. Really, that is one of the best things you can do each and every day. It is easy to be present in the Galapagos, there is so much beauty to take in that you forget about any problems, past or future.

Alexa's Perspective:

After about nine hours of flight, we arrived in Quito. We stepped outside to busy airport traffic and a van that was waiting to take us to our hotel. No one in the group could speak Spanish, but I had taken several Spanish classes in school already. Even at my young age, I could understand bits and pieces and could try to get our thoughts across in very general terms. This bus driver was speaking a thousand miles a minute.

I understood very little, but managed to catch 'hotel' and 'drive.' We all looked at each other, a little worried that we couldn't understand him completely. He was eager for us to get in and go, and we decided to hop in. He drove 80 miles an hour (much over the speed limit for the area) most of the way down the multi-lane road, running red lights and dodging cars left and right. It was a scary way to start the trip, but soon we made it to our beautiful hotel.

We explored the city, where I was quickly convinced to bargain with the vendors on the streets. We walked to a local church and enjoyed seeing Ecuadorian culture along the way. Though some of it was tough to witness, like a small child (probably 2 years old) trying to sell gum, it was mostly incredible to experience a place like this.

We met up with the rest of our crew and the next day we made another short flight to the Galapagos Islands. As far as the eye could see, there was beautiful scenery — trees, ocean water, animals. Our first hotel on the islands had windows from floor to ceiling; you could see the ocean right outside and hear the waves crash against the shore day and night. We had a large room to share as a family. It seemed like a slice of paradise.

Our group was meeting up at a restaurant in the hotel. I hadn't really thought about food and how we might handle eating while preparing for this trip. As we joined our group at the table, I couldn't help but wonder what they might think if I struggled with eating. I didn't know any of the others personally, just mom did, so I wasn't sure how they might react. Would they notice I eat weird? Would they notice I eat slowly? Worst of all, would mom make a big deal about it and embarrass me in front of them all?

I ordered my first chicken strip meal of many, while others were excited to try the local seafood and delicacies of the area. I wasn't one to be adventurous with food, so I was happy when mom said I could stick with something I knew would be yummy. Even the chicken was prepared fresh in-house and was some of the best chicken I've ever eaten. Everyone was busy chatting and enjoying the view and no one noticed a thing about my eating. I was thrilled. Maybe I could relax and enjoy the trip. Mom didn't seem to be focused on food either, so it was a nice change of pace.

The next day, we all met on the shore where I was informed we would be taking a boat ride through the ocean, and that we would be doing this quite often during the trip. For several hours at a time.

I was furious. No one told me there would be this much boating involved. I get motion sick easily and have never enjoyed boats, so I was angry mom didn't inform me about this part of the trip. The rest of our group started singing and laughing and I thought they were crazy. After some convincing, mom and grandma got me on the boat, where I curled into mom's lap, closed my eyes and shoved my fingers in my ears to mute the ocean sounds. Once on the water, it didn't take long for silence to set in. The waves were huge and the ride was rough. But making it to each island and seeing the new sights made it worth it.

The part of the trip I was most excited about was all of the animals we would be seeing. The Galapagos Islands are home to some species that only exist there. I was thrilled to be amongst the small selection of people on planet earth who could say they had seen them in real life. We saw Galapagos tortoises and penguins, blue-footed boobies (yes, that is really what these birds are called), iguanas, sea lions, numerous birds and butter-flies, just to name a few. I was in animal heaven, so everything else seemed to fall away.

Throughout the trip, mom took picture after picture after picture. How could you not with all of this beauty surrounding you? However, there were several times I was eating a snack while we were exploring and mom insisted on taking a picture. In time-sensitive situations like these, I had a hard time swallowing quickly enough to not have food in my mouth for a picture. I would force a mouth-closed smile and try to hide the food in my cheeks. I felt so embarrassed being captured in what I felt was a vulnerable state. I could practically hear the people talking behind my back when they would see the photos, mentioning how weird it was that I had food in my cheeks.

Why couldn't we just wait to take another photo later, or why couldn't we move snack times to when I wouldn't be photographed? It was only a few times though, so I managed a few smiles (I was happy in the moments, just not happy to be captured photographically with food in my mouth) and moved on with the adventures.

My birthday was especially wonderful. That day, we boarded a double-decker boat that took the waves a lot better than the other boats we had been on. We got to see more ocean animals and, to my surprise, on the way back the captain asked me if I wanted to drive the boat. Not only did he let me drive, he went below deck and left me driving solo at the top of the boat. I felt on top of the world!

That evening, we went to a fancy restaurant in the middle of town on the island where we were staying. We ate our meal and just as I thought we were getting ready to be done and leave, a couple of waiters approached from the kitchen carrying a large cake. My heart started pounding with excitement; a cake, for me?!

Everyone sang as the cake arrived at the table. The top was decorated with papaya and other fruits from the island; it was so beautiful. I had never eaten many of the fruits that topped the cake, so I was a little hesitant to take my first bite. I wanted to appreciate and enjoy it, but I was so nervous I would insult the culture if I did not like the cake.

I decided I better take a bite — it was my birthday cake after all — and came to find that I actually really liked it. It was different from any cake I'd had before, but it was delicious and so special. Shortly after that, we met a family who was also celebrating the same birthday as me, 11 years old on the same day. I brought a slice of cake over to the girl and we chatted with her and her family for a while. We exchanged emails so we could keep in touch after the trip. I was excited to have made a friend so unexpectedly and happy I could share some joy through food, which wasn't a normal occurrence for me.

Our ten day trip went by so quickly, but it was the best change of pace from the last several months. We were actually able to relax and enjoy ourselves. I was free amongst my animal friends, mom was entrenched in the nature she so longed to see, and food became an opportunity to learn and bond that it had never been before.

THE BRIDGE

When an immediate family member has an eating disorder, you will need refuge. Water is mine.

We live in the land of 10,000 lakes and many rivers, so we don't have to go far to find water. I think we had two small lakes within five miles of our home, but I wasn't able to seek quick refuge by the lake. We did, however, have a drainage ditch a half mile away, so it was easily accessible. I'm not sure I really knew at the time, but I found a little refuge sitting on the southeast pillar of the bridge, where it crossed the drainage ditch. I went there as much as I could, although never enough. Sometimes, I had time to ride my bike the five miles to the lake. Other times, I could only make it to the drainage ditch for a few moments, just enough to pause and pray, cry and wipe my tears before I went back home.

Almost every time I went, I'd say the same prayer — just give me one more day of strength, I don't think I have it in me. I suppose every day I got back there proved that I was given what I asked for. There, I could breathe, verifying I was still alive. Not completely depleted. I had found a place I could open up and ask for help from God. I was never really able to open up enough to ask for help from others.

Some days I would just watch the water move — taking the attention off of myself and my misery –seeing something that felt more beautiful. A few times I would actually find my way under the bridge near the water's edge where it was easier to hear the water trickle over the rocks or I could watch the occasional school of minnows swim by. The best days were when I'd see turtles sunbathing on nearby branches that had fallen into the ditch.

Often, I just cried. It was a place I could do it in semi-private — except for the occasional car that may have driven by. I usually faced away from the road so they couldn't see me; sometimes, I'd just wave with my hand up high enough to cover my face and show a fake smile.

Some days, it felt like I could fill the ditch with my own tears. I was overwhelmed, stressed and so lonely! I felt helpless — sometimes hopeless, I suppose, in the darkest days. In a way, it was a little like actual grief because it feels like the person with the eating disorder is taking the long way to suicide — slow and painful. And you feel so helpless.

Thinking back, it was probably a mistake for my kids not to see me cry; to see that I break too. I had this crazy belief that if I was seen crying that it meant I was weak. I had every reason to cry — the thought that my daughter could and perhaps even hoped she would be gone. There was also some actual grief in the loss of the little happy, energetic and hopeful girl I'd known her to be. That little girl had disappeared and I had no idea how to get her back.

The river flows and water comes around. I put buckets of tears back into that system and my tears often flow again when I think about those dark times. The ditch gave me answers some days (well, God through my quiet reflection by the ditch) and some days it just held me by letting me know beauty still existed around me. The scenes and sounds of nature were a welcome respite.

When I drive past the bridge now, it takes me back to those days. My body floods with heavy emotion and, almost immediately, the tears flow again. I can practically see myself sitting there in so much pain; I want to jump out and give myself a big hug or just sit beside myself and hold my hand. No words, just someone sitting beside me in support. I also feel the solidness of that corner cement pillar and note how many times it held me. I see the water flowing and my life flowing with it — now in a much better place. Sometimes, I stop by the bridge, sit on that same pillar and express a deep gratitude for having survived — the both of us. I say little prayers for the blessings of the water, the pillar and the small creatures that supported me in this journey.

VENN DIAGRAM

Many things changed after our trip to the Galapagos. I believe it gave me extra strength and confidence because in September that year, I made the difficult decision to pull Alexa from the eating disorder clinic and take her to an Adlerian counselor.

Following the principles of Alfred Adler and Individual Psychology, what makes an Adlerian counselor different is the focus on strengths and uncovering mistaken beliefs. It is more than just talking. It is about finding the strengths and skills that a person already has and using them toward the struggle.

I'd already been seeing my own counselor to help me manage the situation, since I wasn't provided any resources from the clinic. I told him I was frustrated that it didn't seem like Alexa's counselor was getting to the heart of the issue. It just didn't seem like the counselor was able to understand the situation or help.

In one session, the counselor asked us to have a meal in her office. At the end of it, the counselor said how anxious it had made her feel. That was the deciding factor — this wasn't helping and it was time for a change.

When we made the switch, my counselor suggested trying a dual counseling session with one of his female partners. Alexa would see his partner for one hour while I remained working with my counselor at the same time. When our individual times were up, we'd come together to share and discuss further.

I remember coming back together on our first session the most. My counselor and I joined Alexa and her counselor in their room. Alexa was sitting behind a table and you could see a smile and a more confident body posture. Her counselor's face showed excitement and satisfaction as well. Alexa's counselor used the drawing on the whiteboard to walk me through what happened, and encouraged Alexa to chime in.

She had asked Alexa to describe the eating disorder and had placed the words Alexa used on one part of the whiteboard. They were ugly words. Then, she asked Alexa to describe herself; her qualities and interests — what makes her, her. When the descriptions were done, the counselor drew circles around the two and explained to Alexa that there was nothing in common between the two circles; Alexa was not defined by the eating disorder. Apparently, Alexa experienced a big ah-ha moment. At least that's how it seemed to me.

I don't remember sharing what I learned that day. I just remember the change in her expression and posture. Our drive home was more relaxed than it had been in months. I felt a glimmer of hope that we had cracked something open and it felt good. Alexa told me some stories from school and she seemed lighter and a bit more vibrant. Would my little girl come back to me in full? I was hopeful.

We set a date for the next session where they would further explore the eating disorder but, more importantly, set some goals for what she wanted to do in the next 3-6 months. I remember her wanting to do some reading and writing as well as continue training and competing with her dog. There might have even been some art involved. Basically, these were activities that would help Alexa to be herself. She also expressed wanting to handle stress better, to know her triggers but also know what strengths she had to combat them. She also wanted to get better and do more "normal" eating. My goals at that time were to find ways for better communication between us and to help Alexa develop her passions — to find her own life.

Besides setting some forward-looking goals, this process helped us by working with our system. I was part of the system because some of my behaviors were allowing Alexa to "work" the eating disorder. By "work" I mean she knew (consciously or unconsciously) that I would pay more attention and spend more time with her when she was struggling to eat. This was her way to "control" me.

During one of my sessions, I was presented with a graph used to describe the growth of a child. Across the bottom were ages from birth to 18. Up the left side was a list of skills needed to become independent beings. A *line ran diagonally from bottom left, where a baby is fully dependent on its caregivers, to the top right, where the child is fully independent. As children grow, they become more and more capable of the tasks of life. Often, parents continue doing for the child what they are perfectly capable of doing on their own. We think we want to protect our children from some of the struggles we had. But what happens is that we cause harm to their confidence because children start believing the parents think they are incapable.*

I realized that, while I was doing well in many areas, I was probably doing more for my kids than I really should be. I remember Alexa getting mad at me on several occasions because she found out there was an agility competition and I had not signed her up for it. By then, she was perfectly capable of getting online to find the events and note them on a schedule. She was also capable of printing, completing and mailing the registration forms. She already had a checkbook too, so there was no reason that she couldn't write out the checks as well.

Because doing more with her dog was one of her goals, this was easy to use as an opportunity to make her more responsible. She already did a pretty good job caring for her dog, so she was already partly there. But, having her be responsible for the competitions took it to another level.

One of the first things I did was show her the website I used to track events and how to use it to find the type she enjoyed most. There are probably a dozen agility organizations with differing rules, so we mostly chose two organizations that were more beginner friendly. I showed her how to print and then we walked through the first application together. I put together a binder and spreadsheet so she could track events and their results, so she would know which level to register in for each competition.

Once she had the basics, I had to sit back and be quiet. I only gave her a couple of prompts, asking if I needed to add any events to the calendar. From that first week on, I refused to take the blame for not tracking or registering for the agility events. On several occasions, I had to catch myself, wanting to ask if she'd gone online because I felt the urge for her and her dog to have some success. It was hard, but she had to be responsible. It wasn't long before my stress was relieved. It helped Alexa not only see her capability, but also the work it takes to track just this one thing.

When I was getting ready to write this, I asked my counselor what he recalled from that time. He said "I helped you moderate your own concern so that Alexa could step up. Alexa's counselor helped her step up."

When I was able to recognize my part — both some power issues and a little righteousness — and behave as if Alexa was capable of doing the work on her own, it changed the game for both of us.

Today, I tell people I'm an Adlerian because of this experience. I say that the original counselors were just not getting to the underlying issues; they were treating symptoms. What happened here was that we uncovered, together, some mistaken beliefs about who we were and about our relationship as mother and daughter. In a way, I was telling her how to live but then doing some of the work she was capable of doing on her own. In doing so, I was actually hurting her confidence. Once that dynamic changed, everything changed.

My own wellness since those days has improved dramatically. I've since studied Adlerian psychology through classes on human and organizational development, as well as wellness coaching. I now teach workshops on self-care and team wellness, and also provide personal coaching.

It's not that these first few sessions solved all of our problems — it's easy to get caught in old habits. There were plenty more struggles ahead that we had to continually navigate, but these sessions were a major turning point in the path to recovery and our improved relationship.

What I learned is that if my gut says things are not right, it's because they're not right. I am proud that eventually, I did pay attention to my gut and change counselors. I saw how unpacking those underlying beliefs (often mistaken) changed everything about how we moved forward after that. Having counselors provide very specific and attainable actions was something I could sink my teeth into and I didn't have to come up with these actions on my own. Growth and change felt possible.

Another way we were able to use this experience was in Alexa's junior year of high school. Junior year is just a horrible time when adults put such incredible pressure on their kids to decide what they intend to do with the rest of their lives — as if we knew and followed through from our 17-year-old dreams. We want them to decide what work they'll do, what major they'll pursue at just the right college.

Because of the earlier experience, I think Alexa was more open to my suggestion that we go back to my counselor and do an exercise in finding your purpose. We did, and this started the process of finding her calling. She more confidently landed on a major in Anthrozoology at Carroll College, the only school that offered it in the country. Once again — it was getting to the heart that helped her know how to move forward.

I am deeply indebted to the counselors who made a difference in our lives. There's no real way to repay them, other than to let them know how well we are doing now and tell our story so others may benefit.

Alexa's Perspective:

At this point, I had already gone through two therapists at the eating disorder clinic, none seeming to meet my mom's standards. To be fair, I didn't really like them either. It was an awkward hour of sitting across from each other, making small talk and getting nowhere. There was a fakeness in the room that kept all our conversations at a surface level. It felt as if they didn't understand who I was and didn't care to find out. Almost as if I was a checkmark on a list of people they were required to talk to. Sure, I didn't make it easy for them (on account of me not actually wanting to be there or believing I needed to be) and never really opened up, but wasn't it their job to break down those walls?

My mom had been seeing her own therapist at a private practice not far from where I had all of my appointments. Because I wasn't making much progress in my therapy work at the clinic, mom suggested I should try going there as well, even if they didn't necessarily specialize in working with eating disorders. I wasn't thrilled. My experience with therapy thus far had not been great, and if the last two therapists didn't work, why on earth would this one be any different? It would just be another pit stop on the long trek of appointments we already had to go to. But I had no choice in the matter. So, off to a new therapist we went.

Though the building had two stories, it was fairly small. The bottom floor had a bathroom, a lobby area, and not much else. My mom knew the receptionist from her time in therapy and caught up as she filled out paperwork for me. The stairs to the second floor led to a hallway with only a few office areas ducking outward. Mom led us to the first doorway on the right, which opened into another lobby area of sorts. There was a couch, rug, coffee table, and small shelves along the walls with lots of decorations and trinkets to explore. Everything was brown and somewhat dull in appearance, but it created a quiet and calm atmosphere that I didn't mind. The stuffiness of the air, which would usually be annoying and compressing, actually gave a summery-homey feel that went well with the aesthetic. From there, two open doors led to individual office spaces.

"Hi, Michelle." A man emerged from the office on the left. Evidently this was mom's therapist. They greeted each other and quickly turned to me. "This must be Alexa. Nice to meet you." He reached out to shake my hand. I was polite but reserved.

"Sorry, I'll be just another minute!" A woman's voice emerged from the office on the right. Through the process of elimination, I determined she must be my therapist. I wished she would stay hidden and forget about this whole appointment. But to my dismay, about a minute later she emerged from the office space.

"Hi Alexa, I'm Kay. It's so nice to meet you."

"You too." We shook hands and got right to the formalities to get us going.

It was mom's therapist who started us off. "So, I think the plan we had," he nodded to Kay and looked back to my mom and me, "was to talk to each of you individually, separately, and at the end we can join as a group to talk about how it went?"

"I think that sounds great!" My mom happily agreed and I simply nodded my head.

"Well then, Alexa, how about we both head into my office and get started?"

While my inner dialogue was saying 'how about we not,' something in the way Kay's smile was relaxed and her presence was calm and happy, persuaded me to move forward.

Her office was actually much larger than I expected. The left side of the room had a seating area that resembled the lobby; it had several seating options, a center coffee table, and different objects and decorations strung throughout to tinker with or catch your eye. To the right was a long conference-style table with 10 chairs, four on either side and one on each end. The table seemed less intimidating with the large windows along the right wall letting in the natural light and view of the trees outside. The farthest wall from the door, at the far end of the conference table, had a large white-board. At the other end of the table there were baskets on the floor with random objects Kay likely used as part of other sessions.

Kay took her seat on the far side of the conference table, and I chose my seat. I wanted to keep my distance, but not so much distance that it came off as obvious avoidance. I felt small in the large, cushioned chair, but maybe that would help conceal me from what was to come.

Kay began by sharing a little bit about herself and her work to break the ice, but quickly transitioned to focus on me. "Would you mind telling me a little bit about you?"

"Well, I have an eating disorder." I didn't really know what else to say. It was as simple as that. I have an eating disorder, people (aka my mom) think I need help with that, so I was here. That was all there was about me that brought me here.

"Yes, your mom mentioned you were getting some treatment for an eating disorder. That must be hard."

"Yeah."

"But tell me about you, who you are. What makes you, you?" She said it so casually, motioning to me.

I slumped further into my chair, hoping my silence would be an indication to move on to something else. When she kept waiting, I mustered an, "Ummm, I don't know…"

"Having an eating disorder isn't a trait about you. Let's try something." She got up from her seat, walked over to the whiteboard, and picked up a dry-erase marker. "Do you like writing on whiteboards? We're going to try a Venn diagram exercise. Do you want to write, or do you want me to write?"

I wasn't sure where this was going, but I actually did enjoy writing on whiteboards. "I can do it."

"Good," she passed me the dry-erase marker and went back to her seat. "You can start by drawing a large circle. It should be pretty big. Then draw another circle about the same size to the right of it but overlap them so there are three sections total. One section in just the left circle, one section that is part of both circles, and one section in just the right circle." I drew the circles as she asked, then stood back to wait for what was next. "Now put your name above the left circle. And how about for the right circle, we label it Ed, like E-D, short for eating disorder."

I thought it was a little weird she wanted to give an eating disorder a name, but I did as she asked and stepped back again. "Ok, now we can start filling it in. Let's start with the left side. In the left section, put any words that you think describe you."

I turned around to face the circles and raised the marker to the board. I shimmied myself closer, my face mere inches from the board, waiting for inspiration to strike and my hand to start moving. But nothing happened. I froze. It was as if all of my vocabulary had disappeared into thin air. I felt heat rise in my chest from embarrassment and anxiousness that I couldn't conjure the answers she wanted, and tears started to well up in my eyes.

Kay gave me a minute or so to stand and take in what she had asked, but when I didn't respond, she chimed in. "Can you think of any words to put in your circle?" I shook my head, not sure what to do next. "Maybe I can help start us out. How about creative — are you creative?"

I pondered it for a second. As a matter of fact, I actually was. I was a little surprised how she would know that when we just met but decided not to question it. "Yeah, I do art camps with my friend Macy during the summer."

"Ok great, let's put 'creative' in your circle." I wrote the word and felt a spark of hope and excitement. Finally, there was something on the board. "What else?" She put the ball back in my court, but this time instead of freezing with uncertainty, words started coming to me.

"Lots of people say I'm smart."

"Ok, awesome! Smart is another great trait, add it to the circle!"

"I'm friendly and caring." I started writing the words down in a list on the 'Alexa' side of the circle. Words started coming to my mind at a steady pace — words like silly, authentic, intuitive, family-oriented and animal-lover. I could see Kay smiling from the corner of my eye, and something about her encouragement made me believe she was actually curious to learn these things about me. She was smiling about the real me.

After I filled most of the left side of the circle, Kay chimed in. "That's great, Alexa. I'm glad we got a good list in your circle. How about we switch over to ED's side now?"

"Sure." I took a step over to the other circle, not exactly sure how to start.

Kay didn't wait to help me out this time, she jumped right in with some instructions. "Think about your eating disorder as another person in the room. What do they do to you and how does it make you feel?"

I tried to picture it, pretending I was eating a meal right now in my mind. "It makes me feel lonely."

"That's a good observation. I'll help you write these down as characteristics a person might have, instead of how you feel. You can keep telling them to me that same way, but I'll help you rephrase them to characteristics or traits. Let's put that in the circle as 'isolator.' What else is ED like?"

"It makes me feel like I don't have any control."

"Ok, let's write that down as 'controller.'"

I again started to accumulate a list with Kay's support — attention-seeker, liar, and depressor to name a few. I could feel my confidence in this exercise rise as the board began to fill.

"This is great work, Alexa. Now let's look at the middle section, where the 'Alexa' circle and 'ED' circle overlap. Are there any words you can think of that fit both you and ED?"

I glanced at the words on my side, and then at the words on ED's side. All of these words seemed quite different from each other. I tried hard to think of something to add to the middle, hoping Kay wouldn't be disappointed that I again needed help getting started. To my surprise, I got a different reaction.

"You can't think of any words for the middle that describe you and ED?"

"No..."

"I don't think I can either. That's because you are not ED. You are not your eating disorder." She pointed to the circle labeled 'Alexa.' "You are all of these amazing things — creative, smart, silly — and ED is something that is not any of those things. ED is trying to take over and pretend to be Alexa, but you are <u>you</u>."

I had never looked at it that way before.

All this time it seemed having an eating disorder was the only thing people cared about. But that wasn't me, it was something happening to me right now. I was still me deep down, even if ED was trying to hide it. And ED was doing a pretty good job up until now because, honestly, I had forgotten what the real me looked like.

Kay let me sit with this for a few minutes, then we transitioned to talking about some of my specific struggles and actionable steps to work on those. I was much more open with her now that I knew she cared about me, the real me, and our time together flew by. When it was time to come together as a group, mom and her therapist came over to Kay's office (it was a bigger space for all of us to gather). I could already see an inquisitive look on mom's face.

"How was your time together?" Kay asked them both as they entered.

"Good, as always, lots more to think about," mom looked to her counselor to watch him smile and nod in agreement. As mom sat down, she pointed to the whiteboard which still held my diagram. "I'm curious to hear what this is all about." She wore a look of surprise and hopefulness, settling into her chair with the energy of a kid waiting for a treat but visibly trying to stay collected and calm.

"Yes, we had some good conversation too," Kay replied. "Alexa, would you like to share a little about what that diagram is?" Suddenly, I got nervous to see their reactions. How dumb would it sound that I barely knew who I was?

I pointed to the diagram as I responded, "We put words that describe me in this circle, and then words that describe my eating disorder in this circle."

"And Alexa had a little bit of a tough time starting out thinking of words to fill in, but once she got going it went well, didn't it Alexa?" Kay added.

"Yeah." I was avoiding my mom's eyes and tried to stay focused on Kay. "Then we tried to think of words to put in the middle that fit me and ED, but neither of us could think of any."

Kay explained more about how we called the eating disorder 'ED' and how this helped show that the eating disorder was like someone else trying to hurt me, but I was separate and had the power to fight back against ED.

Mom listened very intently to Kay and nodded her head in approval, "Wow, that's exactly right. I'm glad it went so well." We transitioned to talk a little about what mom had discussed with her therapist before wrapping up for the day.

"I think this went really well," mom's therapist remarked. "Let's head downstairs and we can set up another time to do this again, if that's what you both want?"

"Absolutely, thank you so much," mom answered.

I didn't have much say in the matter, but for the first time since this eating disorder started, I actually didn't mind having to come back. Things I loved about myself and about my life had been brought back to the surface when they had been buried for so long.

A glimpse of hope reappeared. Maybe I was strong enough to do this. After all, I was already a fighter (sometimes not in the best ways), so if I directed my fight where it belonged, just maybe I could make it out of this struggle.

CLIMBING OUT

The following months still had their difficult moments. Some foods were still a battle, some days I ate slower than others, and some days mom still frustrated me. But slowly, I started to improve. My meal timer decreased from an hour to forty-five minutes, to half an hour. My weight steadily climbed. I was getting better.

My mindset had shifted. Before, everything that was wrong was because of me. I was the freak who couldn't complete such a basic human task as eating. I was the girl who was so unlovable and strange that no one understood me. I was the one who caused and desired screaming matches and a good fight. But it wasn't me the whole time. It was "ED."

Now, I knew ED was separate from me, a completely different being who was influencing my life. ED was whispering in my ear that I couldn't eat another bite, that I would choke, that I didn't like this food or that food. ED was putting himself in front of me as a mask to others, not allowing them to see the true me. ED was holding a curtain over my reflection, not allowing me to really know myself either. ED was puppeting my hands and heart, starting fights I never wanted to happen.

Now that he was exposed, I could begin to fight back. It wasn't me fighting mom or her fighting me, it was us fighting ED. Together. Does this mean we got along perfectly? No, of course not. And, of course, it took a while to solidify and strengthen this new mindset. But we could start to recognize my internal dialogue from ED, correct the false narrative, and act against him. I had to tell myself things like "you like apples, ED is saying that you don't, but you do," and "you are confident, ED is saying you are scared, but you are not," and "you've only had a couple bites, you can't be full, ED says you are full, but you are not."

Eventually, I reached the goal weight that the medical professionals had set for me. Our appointments became less frequent until they stopped.

Throughout my struggle, when I yearned to be done with all the chaos, I had imagined some grand celebration from the clinic at the end of it all. Something that said, "you're cured!" I imagined music playing and providers throwing their hands in the air as they escorted me to the front door for the final time. But there was none of that. Providers completed their part of the appointments as normal and sent me out, and we exited the building amongst the normal bustle of the lobby. Very anticlimactic. Almost as if they expected me to return. Or that what I had done was easy, just another day at the office.

At home, many of the rules and routines continued. Meal planning, general timing of meals, vigilance of my actions during meals. So even though I was "recovered" there was never the definitive ending or reset that I had hoped for all along. There was much less pressure, but something told me my life would never go back to what it was before. Mom would always be concerned about my eating and life habits, even if she didn't outwardly express it or if she tried to hide her watchful eye. I would have to be satisfied with the bit of relief I got from being separated from a treatment facility. I slowly regained mom's trust, but I always felt the worry in the back of her mind.

Despite the slight awkwardness of the transition from eating disorder to remission, we had to be proud. ED tried to take me down, take mom down, take us down, but we won. If he tried to come back and fight some more, we were better prepared to defeat him. This would likely be one of the hardest things we would ever have to go through, if not the very hardest. It was hell. But we climbed out.

Mom's Perspective:

We had to keep the rules as a part of trust building. Slowly, Alexa could make more decisions about food. Meal planning still happened. I started giving Nick and Alexa recipe cards or a list of favorite recipes to make some of our meal choices for the weekly menu. Not only was it a way to keep her eating as she should, but it also kept me from hearing the dreaded "Ugh" when asking what was for supper when they came home from school.

Sometimes, we'd even make the meals together. It was during that time that we began to play with more recipes as well — to expand the palette and find more foods that the kids might like (and incorporate when they eventually went out on their own). There were a few meals that Alexa really liked but Nick didn't so much. I think of Beans and Franks Chowder. Nick wasn't a fan, but he tolerated it — I suspect in an effort to help out his sister the way she often did for him.

I think some of the remaining fights we had during this time could have been teenage rebellion creeping in. I can't imagine what this fight would have been like had it started in those early teenage years. It was hell the way it was at ages 10-12. I'm not sure I would have survived. Or Alexa probably would have ended up as an in-patient client instead.

When we reached the goal weight about seven or eight months after starting our journey, I remember sitting in the doctor's office; Alexa had a smile on her face and some sense of accomplishment. I remember feeling a small release of the stress on my body. I knew, though, that just because we had reached our goal, this fight wasn't over. Alexa was still growing and that meant her goal weight would keep climbing. So, the food amounts might even have to increase to keep up. We stopped at KFC and DQ on the way home, which is strange that we would celebrate with food. That's why the eating disorder didn't make so much sense sometimes.

I also couldn't let my guard down. Who knows what might be the next trigger to take her backwards. This experience was so painful, there was no way I would let it creep back in again. I wasn't as vigilant but I also was quite protective of her and me. I saw what a lack of nutrition did for her brain and personality — much less her body. I couldn't risk anything.

By the time Alexa met her goal weight, we had already started to decrease the time set on the timer. We were already at 45 minutes and heading toward 30. It was probably another six months or so before we could *remove the timer all together. Once or twice, there were short dust ups and I had to bring it back out again.*

Once we got Alexa back, it was easier to talk to each other without blame. Her separation from the eating disorder was slowly becoming complete. I would explain to people back then that it felt like multiple personality disorder; there were times it was clear when Alexa had left the room and ED had taken over. When that Alexa spark disappeared, I knew there would be a fight. Thankfully, those fights began to diminish greatly and eventually subsided completely.

Changing Seasons

ON THE MOVE

My parents got divorced during the time we were navigating my eating disorder. The day they decided to tell my brother and me about their decision to part ways, I could feel the reality setting in before the words ever left their mouths. We were coming home from church and pulling into the driveway when my mom turned around toward the backseat.

"Let's all meet in the living room when we get inside, your dad and I want to sit down and talk with both of you."

I don't know exactly how, but immediately in my head I told myself 'They're getting divorced.' I felt like a heavy drape was laid over me as I slowly took a step out of the van, my mind racing and blank at the same time. I was mostly worried about what Nick would think, how he would feel, but I didn't necessarily feel a sense of doom.

After a little bit of family chaos, we sat down to have my inner voices confirmed. My parents were indeed getting a divorce. Dad would be moving out while mom stayed in this house. But we'd still see them both, and go to the same school, and it was not our fault this was happening. And for a while, all of that was true.

Dad moved in with his parents across the street and decided to start building a new house just down the road. It was small, but cozy. Nick and I spent some days staying with dad (and my grandparents while he was still building the "little house" as we called it) and some days with mom. Our school lives continued on as normal. Since the houses were so close the bus had no problem dropping us off at either dad's or mom's. Of course, we were coping with our family not being a cohesive unit under one roof and with being kids trying to understand how this could happen and what it would mean, but everything stayed pretty ok.

As I got older and further removed from my eating disorder, mom opened up more with me. Naturally, conversations eventually turned to what led to my parents' divorce. To be honest, neither of my parents ever really tore down the other after the divorce. They both acted civil, friendly even, to stay supportive for both us kids. However, mom's first response was usually the same — "your dad didn't help with your eating disorder."

Sure, there were other reasons to follow. But whenever mom shared this primary reason, I couldn't help but think if I never had an eating disorder our family would still be intact. If not for me, they wouldn't have had to disagree so much, and they wouldn't have felt like they needed to get a divorce. It was all mine and ED's fault.

Over the course of two years, mom dated and decided to re-marry. We relocated two hours away from dad, limiting our visits with him to weekends. New home, new school, new "family." I was not thrilled.

As we made the move, even though I wasn't in the deepest depths of struggling with my eating disorder, I couldn't help but wonder how this new guy and his three sons would react to seeing me eat. What if I struggled and mom made a big deal about it? What if they ate a bunch of foods I didn't like? What if they watched me eat and thought I was weird? Even though I was recovered for the most part, I still didn't feel "normal." My family had gotten used to my struggles at this point, but encountering new people and having to explain myself always worried me.

Though I'm sure they did judge me from time to time, I don't remember any specific instances where I was called out or felt particularly judged for my eating. But that worry translated to meeting other new people as well. As I started meeting new friends in school and got invited over to people's houses, in my teens as I started dating, meeting new families always raised my anxiety. Not because I was worried about what they would think of me, I liked to think I could get along with most people, but because I was worried they would notice my eating.

Throughout middle and high school, my eating disordered past was something I felt I needed to keep hidden. Surely no one would be able to look at me the same if they knew I couldn't even eat right, a basic human function. Moving to a new place, at the very least, was an opportunity to start over with no one knowing my past, so I was determined to keep it all a secret.

Mom's Perspective:

What I remember most about moving was a conversation we had one day on the way to practice or some school event in the late afternoon. I was still seeing my own therapist at the time — attempting to recover myself from all that had happened. We talked about my fears about Alexa's eating disorder during the move. He suggested that I just ask directly about what fears Alexa and Nick might have in moving.

So, as we were driving and in a moment of silence, I told Alexa I wanted to ask her something. Alexa said okay, though I could see a little apprehension in her face. I asked what fears might be coming up about the move. She didn't have to think long and said two things quite quickly. First, that she was scared to lose her friends. Second, that she was afraid that she wouldn't see her dad.

First, I told her Macy was one of those friends that never leaves — even through great distance and time. I know because I have those kinds of friends from grade school. Even though we lost touch for a while, when we began getting together again, it was like we were never apart. In fact, it was even better because we had matured. I felt like Macy was a person I wanted her to keep forever. I love Macy and her family as much as Alexa does, so this was a no-brainer. I shared that I was starting over in some ways with friends as well. We could both do our best to keep these solid friendships in our lives.

For the second, I told Alexa that she could come back to Dad's EVERY weekend if she wanted. We would have to make sure it would work with school activities and my travel, but I would do everything I could to make sure her connection to her dad stayed intact (and, of course, Nick's too). I said I had no intention of taking them from their father.

I remember watching Alexa's body kind of relax as she heard what I had to say. I was as truthful as I could be without overcommitting to anything.

And she felt it. It was one of the first conversations that felt really connected in a long time — even though it was a hard conversation to have.

There were a few instances leading up to the move when ED raised its ugly head. I think it was, in part, an attempt to break us up so there was no move. After our talk, the rest of the move was typical to how moves go.

I was a little worried about the new school. It was much bigger than any the kids attended in the past, so there was a good possibility they could both get lost in the shuffle. I did my best to make the transition as painless as possible for everyone involved.

SIGNS OF SURVIVAL

In the summer before Alexa's first year of high school, Nick and Alexa went to stay with my younger brother and his family in Illinois. They spent about half the summer there. They got to spend time with their cousins, who were all relatively similar in age. They worked together detasseling corn and playing on evenings and weekends. They got to earn some money, but also got to see another family dynamic and that is cool. Plus, they both experienced a change from the way we do things in our family. I believe it was nice for both of them to get a break from me. It was also a way for me to show I trusted them both outside our home, including with meal issues.

I was worried that high school, at some point, might send Alexa into a relapse. That can be a tough time for anyone. There were several signs and events that showed me things would be okay, however. First, Alexa joined Nick's bowling team to help them out and she was the only girl on the team. Since she was traveling with us to competitions, it was easy for her to bowl instead of just watch.

She started track in eighth grade and that carried over into high school.

But music was where Alexa really seemed to find her people and met most of her close friends through the high school's amazing music programs. I think those friends were a major factor in navigating high school without any major flair ups.

I also think her activities helped her maintain regular eating. Marching band started in ninth grade. A rigorous two-week program started in mid-August before the school year officially started. That band camp was followed by early morning practices every day in the fall. It was a lot of physical work and the uniforms were heavy on competition days. Alexa always carried more snacks than needed for those days. When we rode home together from competitions, we stopped at restaurants. While Alexa still wasn't the fastest eater, I was confident she was getting the calories she needed.

Alexa survived her first real boyfriend during her junior year of high school as well. They seemed happy together. When things turned a little south after some months, she stood up for herself and broke up with him. She was a little sad but recovered quickly. I was so proud of her.

When the bowling alley closed, Alexa and her friends could have easily quit the team. They did not. Instead, they pursued other nearby bowling alleys for sponsorship. They found a first and then a second over the final years before graduation. Persistence was developing strongly within her.

I knew she was tough when she joined speech her freshman year. Any kid who can take the (often harsh) feedback from judges in practice and competition, is impressive. I believe if a kid can survive speech and its continuous feedback, they are probably going to make great employees.

She never gave up. I was most proud of Alexa when she decided to bring her eating disorder into her senior year's persuasive speech. By then, she'd been slowly sharing that struggle with a couple of close friends. Now the entire school could potentially hear what it was about. I was inwardly hoping it would go deeper into the struggle than it did, but it was out there, nonetheless. I knew that the eating disorder and the shame that goes along with it had nowhere to hide anymore.

I remember the first time I heard it in public. I was sitting in the audience, but I had to keep my head down. I suspected I might get emotional and I didn't want to throw her off her game. I shed a couple of tears, but I couldn't let her see my face. There were so many emotions — I was so proud of her for showing up fully.

Alexa had a bit of a dilemma that final season. She wanted her speech to do well but she had spent four years building up and holding on to the bowling team. Bowling competitions were always the same weekend as speech. She chose to split her time — sometimes missing bowling and sometimes missing speech. Even only showing up half of the season, Alexa made it to the state competition in both activities.

During high school she volunteered to be a freshman mentor for two years. She was also a homework helper at the middle school for several years.

I saw that she knew what she wanted and went for it all. That is a skill that I still work on at times. It is one that will serve her well for her whole life. If she dreams it, I know she can make it happen.

One final event that solidified her recovery for me was when I volunteered to do a self-inquiry activity for the local church youth group. After the activity concluded, there was a short discussion period. I don't recall what the question was, but I do remember telling them Alexa had suffered from an eating disorder when she was younger. I said I could say that now that she was openly mentioning it in speech. Afterward the youth director told me one of the students asked her if she thought it would be ok to reach out. I said she could absolutely reach out to me and that I'd talk to Alexa to get permission too. I told Alexa and she did not hesitate to grant permission for the reach out. Perhaps that was the first time she was open to helping others. I don't think the student ever reached out to her, but at least they knew they were not alone.

The eating disorder could no longer hide. I think EDs want shame to rule to make it easier to control their humans. Alexa had become a strong and resilient fighter, and ED was no longer in control.

Alexa's Perspective:

I think many people look back on high school saying they would never go back, but I honestly enjoyed high school. I made the most out of my time by joining as many activities as I could fit into my schedule and enjoying life with my friends. Sure, there was some drama every now and then, but that's to be expected.

During one of the middle years of my high school experience, a girl in my class shared a social media post about her struggle with an eating disorder. I had no idea she was struggling. Suddenly, other girls in my class were reaching out to show their support for her and thanked her for sharing her story because they could relate. This was one of the first times I realized that maybe I didn't have to hide or be ashamed of my past eating disorder. Maybe there were more people out there struggling, and my story could help them feel less alone, too.

So, my senior year, I decided to take a leap of faith and share some of my story publicly. I asked my speech coach if we could write something that incorporated my eating disorder. He was happy to help me through the process. I was successful that season, not only in winning awards for my speech, but in being courageous and open with my story. Little did I know, that would be just the start for me.

I could still sense the worry in the back of mom's mind. Even though I recovered from my eating disorder, she was still watchful and cautious. Part of me knew it would always be this way. I understood why it was scary for her. For both of us. But part of me also wanted to be fully separated. I didn't want food or weight to always be a concern. I knew better how to take care of myself now, and I wished she could trust that.

OPENING UP

During my junior year, we had to take a careers class to help determine what job we might want in the future and to figure out where we might like to apply for college. I always knew I wanted to help people and I had always been very intuitive to the needs of people around me. Becoming a counselor or therapist seemed like a logical next step, but I wasn't quite sure. When I did some searching and discovered the up-and-coming incorporation of animal-assisted interventions to this field, I knew this was the path for me. Cisco, along with many other animals, had been a form of therapy for me throughout my life. If I could share this with others in a structured way, it felt like the right calling.

There was also a rise in people on social media sharing their stories of struggling with mental health and the world was shifting to support them instead of criticizing or shaming them. What if my struggle with an eating disorder was supposed to be used to help others? What if sharing my story could influence someone else? What if that was the whole point all along?

What if my struggle wasn't for nothing?

I had always enjoyed writing as a kid. I wrote short stories about animals and illustrated each page to match the story. I came up with elaborate plans for novels and started writing a few chapters, but none of the stories ever became more than just a hobby for me. However, I decided maybe writing was where I needed to start with my eating disorder journey.

I thought back to one of the events most ingrained in me during my eating disorder struggle. It was the story of a girl I met who shared her bracelets with me, but was doomed to die by those around her. I started writing.

At first, I was thinking a blog would be good. People were into blogs, right? I completed that blog post along with one other but, as I wrote, I doubted whether this would be helpful to anyone. What if I exposed myself with all of these stories and it ended up not being useful to anyone?

Even though I didn't really want to share this with mom, she was too involved in the stories. I couldn't think of anyone else who might be able to say whether this was a good idea or not. I told her my plan and offered to have her read the first piece of writing. We were both nervous in the process. I thought for sure she would get upset about how I portrayed her. But, as she read through, she surprisingly validated me and told me she thought it was a great idea.

We had a conversation about that day at the conference and what she remembered. Though it brought up a lot of sad feelings, (I think we both cried), it also allowed our perspectives to mesh and helped us grow closer even though we were so distant then. We started to consider that maybe this was OUR story.

It also made me realize that maybe sharing my story could result in the opposite of what I had anticipated. Maybe it could bring perspective and help people grow closer together. Maybe it could bring relationships and healing just from being able to relate.

School started; enjoying my senior year, along with finding a college, took my focus and my writing went on pause. Through my searches on animal-assisted interventions, I found a college in Montana that offered both a robust psychology program and a human-animal program unlike any other in the country. After some internal debate, I decided I was supposed to go there and double major in both.

I wasn't thrilled about how far I would be from home, but I decided to view it as an adventure out west. Like many pioneers before me, I was moving west to jumpstart my dreams. In reality, it was much less glorious than that, but it kept me focused on enjoying the moment even when I missed home.

The first days and weeks of college I was terrified, but tried to put myself out there to meet new friends. My roommate and I quickly bonded over our love of animals (she was doing the same human-animal major that

I was), and our next-door neighbors, two girls from Washington, quickly became some of my great friends as well.

Thoughts in the back of my mind kept turning to the fear of sharing. I finally decided now was probably as good a time as any to share and see what happens. One day I visited my neighbors' dorm room, we relaxed and chatted, sharing a little bit about ourselves and getting to know each other on a more personal level. I decided to mention my eating disorder and how I wanted to write about it.

To my surprise, they both related and shared their own struggles with eating in the past as well. I was so grateful for their willingness to share, not to mention that we each found a support system during that transition into college that we didn't know we needed, or at least I didn't.

Though our schedules didn't always align, one of them and I often went to the dining hall together. We were always willing to stay as long as the other needed to feel comfortable eating and not be left alone and vulnerable. It was something simple, as I remembered Macy doing so long ago, but it felt just as special. Maybe opening up wasn't so bad. In fact, maybe it was the open door to healing.

Mom's Perspective:

I feel bad for high school juniors. That is the year they are pressured into making their ultimate life decision. There is a bunch of pressure to decide a career and college path. Just the summer before, Nick, Alexa and I went on a three-state, multi-college tour in preparation for Nick going off to college. Once he found Actuarial Science, he knew exactly what he wanted to do. I think when Alexa reached her junior year, she was really unsure. I had a sneaking suspicion she was mentally struggling with it. Not that she didn't know anything about what she wanted to do, but more so that she had so many interests she was lost in which direction to take.

I had attended a business workshop hosted by my counselor and seen him do a purpose exercise. I told Alexa I'd be willing to pay for a session with him so she could hone in on her purpose. She said she would be interested and I made the appointment. I asked if she wanted me in the room with her or in the waiting room. She wanted me there.

I remember sitting at the end of the table farthest away from the counselor and sort of to the side of Alexa so at least, at times, I'd be out of view. She needed to do the work and not look to me for any answers or guidance. This was an exercise to find HER passions, not be influenced by mine or what I thought.

After getting to know each other a bit, the counselor started doing his thing. He asked about things Alexa loved to do, what she was good at and what types of jobs she already thought she might be interested in. As I've learned from him, purpose often lies in the minus you see in the world that you want to change to a plus.

He started drawing on the whiteboard. Alexa knew she wanted to do something with animals. Not just that she loved them, but she saw how much Cisco did for her during her deepest struggle. She also said she wanted to help people. We didn't get to the final purpose that day, but it did give Alexa more direction on where to look.

At that point, she started to search more about careers that involved both people and animals. Then she started searching for schools. Eventually, she landed on three that had programs with an animal component and a people component, although they were each very different. They were located in Pennsylvania, Montana and Wisconsin. We visited the one in Pennsylvania first. Although their equestrian barn was pretty cool, I remember the tone of the school being a little princess-like. It didn't feel like a place where she would be comfortable.

We had a lovely visit to Montana and learned more about the Anthrozoology program. What really excited Alexa about the program was that, during junior year, students could take a dog from the shelter, train it for a service and then hand it over to someone who needed that service. If that went well, they could get their own dog to train for whatever purpose they wanted. That there was potential to have a pet and train while going to school was pretty exciting. We also got to speak directly with the head of the program at that time — a leader in the field. The school was also smaller in size and its western, more casual tone, felt more like home.

We did visit the school in Wisconsin but, by that time, she had pretty much made up her mind that she'd be going to Montana. This school would have had to knock her socks off to make the final cut.

OWN YOUR TRUTH

Though I found friends and support, there were still times I struggled to share and struggled to fit in with my eating. Even though the depths of my eating disorder were years ago, it still sometimes required attention. One such time was the first big holiday during my college experience; Thanksgiving.

While many students were headed back to their families for the holidays, my family was several states away and I couldn't afford to travel back for every school break. Especially when the next break was only a few weeks away and I would be going home then, I stayed on campus. Luckily for me, there were a select few other students also staying for the holiday and a few gracious professors in my department decided to host a Thanksgiving meal.

The meal would be hosted in our department's house. The house was on campus but looked like one a family or group of roommates might typically live in. It had a kitchen, a living room, a bathroom and some bedrooms. The only things distinguishing it from any other house were the sign the department put out front, the mounds of animal supplies in the basement and the animal decor splayed across the walls and counter space. Our department used the building for animal classes, projects, and a cozy place to study and meet with people of similar interests. It wouldn't be hard to transform the space to host a Thanksgiving dinner.

I walked in that day to find several students and professors had already arrived. We chatted and passed time waiting for all of the guests. Everyone brought something to share and we ended up with a pretty large spread. There were foods many of us had never tried before along with Thanksgiving classics. I was excited to mingle and explore new foods, but I didn't want to stand out. Whether it was eating slowly or not liking certain foods, I didn't want to be noticed. I told myself I would take small portions of a little bit of everything to meet in the middle. What could go wrong? When it was time to eat, we all took our places at the table.

"Everyone pass your plates down and I'll serve up the turkey," one of the professors announced. My heart dropped. The professor grabbed my plate and cut off two large slabs of turkey. This was way more than I planned on eating. Honestly, it was much more than most of the others around me would probably eat, given all the other options available to try on the side.

I had become more comfortable in college with feeding myself; I allowed myself to try new things and eat what was provided, but also gave myself grace now and then. I had snacks stocked up in my dorm room to supplement if I was rushed to get somewhere after a meal or if the food wasn't my favorite. And honestly, in social situations, I still felt some pressure when eating, feeling like others would judge me, so I liked to have a back-up option where I could eat alone and not worry.

But at Thanksgiving, there is an expectation that you eat a bunch of food.

My thoughts started racing. Maybe no one would notice I didn't finish everything. Maybe I could come up with something else. Maybe I could say I had eaten before this. But why would I do that when I knew I was coming here?

A few days prior I wasn't feeling very good. Maybe I could say I was still recovering and hadn't gotten my full appetite back yet.

Or, an even wilder thought, what if I was completely honest and just explained that it was not the portion I had planned for? I could elaborate on my past if needed. Or maybe I would get lucky and no one would say anything at all.

I tried to blend into the mealtime conversations. But though I enjoyed the people and the food, I was uneasy and uncomfortable. What I pictured being a relaxing time had been tainted by my own eating insecurities. I'm not sure whether that showed, or whether my intuition was right, but the turkey-serving professor spoke up.

"Alexa, didn't you like the turkey? Am I that bad of a cook?" The professor elbowed my arm in a joking manner.

"Oh no, the food is all amazing!" Suddenly I could feel the other eyes on me. I quickly reviewed all the options in my head for how to respond. "I actually haven't been feeling the greatest the past few days. I'm feeling better now but still not quite back to my regular appetite." Small remarks of pity circled around the table. I reassured everyone I was fine and that I enjoyed the food and their willingness to share the holiday.

Later on, as I sat and thought in the solitude of my dorm room, I couldn't help but be angry at myself for not speaking my truth. For reverting back to my younger ways of hiding my struggles and insecurities instead of being honest. But the moment had passed and I couldn't change it. I would just have to use this as an example to myself for the future. I had shared before with only positive outcomes so, next time, I told myself, I would change my narrative.

REMNANTS

It was almost exactly a year later when I would be confronted with my eating disorder again, but in a much different way.

My sophomore year, I took a job working at my college's horse barn. I loved it. It was a few hours in the mornings or afternoons where I could escape campus, get outside, and hang out with some cool animals. I often shared pictures or stories with my roommates, so I was excited when one of them asked if she could tag along to see what I do and meet the horses. I offered to drive us out to the barn and warned her that the tag-along would include chores before getting to chill with the horses. She didn't mind at all and was just excited to share in the experience.

We greeted my coworker upon arrival and headed to the feed station to do our first task — getting the horses' breakfast ready. The section of the barn for preparing feed was set up like a workstation. There was a long, metal table that held the bowls, supplements, and medications. The table also had a shelf underneath, where bins of different types of feed were kept. A whiteboard hung on the wall, listing feeding and tack details for each horse. On the other side of the space, stacks of hay bales lined the walls. Every feeding time, I would line up the bowls on the table to correspond with the names on the whiteboard and start by filling each bowl with the correct type and amount of feed. Then I would go through and add supplements to the bowls that needed it.

On this day, I was so excited to show my roommate around that I started filling the bowls a little quicker than normal, bending down and standing up as fast as I could. When I stood up from the third scoop, my vision suddenly went black. The blackness only lasted a second, then transitioned to static before finally returning to normal. At the same time, my heart began beating out of my chest at what felt like a million beats per minute. My whole upper chest was purring and pounding at the same time and I was lightheaded. I stumbled back to sit on the hay bales. My roommate and coworkers both noticed and asked if I was ok.

Unfortunately, this had happened before; once during seventh grade basketball practice, twice during high school track and one other time at college. I had gone to the doctor after the episodes, only to be told nothing was wrong with me. I explained this to my roommate and coworker and told them it usually only lasted a few minutes. I tried not to stress. I focused on my breathing and talked with them to try to occupy my mind.

After almost ten minutes went by with no signs of stopping, I started to get worried. All I could think to do was call my mom. She tried to reassure me but also expressed concern for how long this episode was lasting. I asked if I should go to the emergency room. She said she couldn't really say since she wasn't there to see what was happening, so I should use my best judgment. I hung up with her, and told my roommate if it lasted another five minutes, I should probably go to get checked out. I was still trying to stay calm, but deep down, these episodes always scared me.

Five minutes later, nothing had changed. My roommate backed my vehicle into the barn to pick me up and we headed to the nearest emergency room, which was about ten minutes away. We walked into the waiting room and explained the situation. The receptionist asked for my information and had me start filling out paperwork. She paged a nurse to bring a finger tester out to determine my heart rate and oxygen level. Right before the nurse came out, I felt the pressure return to my head and, in what felt like a large wave, my heartbeat returned to normal. Though I was relieved, I was a little upset that we just went through all this trouble to get to the ER and now it was over. Again, it would likely appear to the medical professionals that nothing was wrong, even though I knew something was not right.

They took me back to do some testing anyway, including drawing my blood. Due to my extreme discomfort with needles, I asked if my roommate could come along. I don't know whether it was the skill of the nurse, my pride in not wanting to be embarrassed in front of my friend, or my friend's distraction with conversation, but it was the fastest and most pain-less blood draw I had ever experienced. I was so grateful to have my friend there at the barn that day. But suddenly, it sunk in that I had ruined our barn adventure for the day. I promised my roommate I would take her again on a different day.

The doctor came in with a few more questions and then, to my sur-prise, offered a possible diagnosis. They said based on my descriptions of the times these episodes had occurred, along with my history of an eating disorder, it was likely orthostatic hypotension. They described it as a mis-communication between my brain and body, causing my blood pressure to rapidly change, which would cause the symptoms I was experiencing. It all seemed to make sense, and they gave some recommendations for how to avoid it in the future, so I left that day with a little bit of relief.

However, it didn't take long for a little bit of anger to creep in. Even though I was so much healthier now, my eating disorder still found ways to linger in my life. While this was a quick ER visit and not an official diag-nosis, the fact that it could potentially be related to my past eating disorder was scary. I never would've thought that the effects of my eating disorder could persist later into my life. I was mad at myself for ever having an eating disorder and I was sad at the fact that I may have to deal with the impacts and reminders my entire life.

I tried not to blame myself. I had to be grateful for the fact that there were things I could do to prevent this problem in the future. Though I was frustrated, I had to remind myself it was a blessing to be here even if it came along with a few medical hiccups. The impacts of my eating disorder could have been much worse. And I had to remind myself that I didn't cause my eating disorder. I fought it and beat it as best I could. And I would keep winning no matter what was thrown my way.

Mom's Perspective:

I remember taking the call from Alexa that day. It was late afternoon and I was working, but thankfully not in the middle of a workshop or an important meeting. I picked up the phone with our usual banter — 'hola, mi hija!' (we pretend we can speak Spanish sometimes). She calmly described that she was having another heart episode. My heart sank into my chair and she had my full attention. By the time she called me, the issue had already gone on for about twelve minutes.

I recall one time in track when she was running hurdles. I could see as soon as she left the starting blocks that something wasn't right. As she took the first corner, I could see her really struggling to get her legs over the hurdles and her stride just wasn't there. When I asked her what happened, she told me her heart started racing before the blocks but, because she was only in two events that day, she didn't want to drop out for the team.

I was a little upset about that. But it was a short episode.

I asked if she was sitting down and if anyone else was with her in the barn. I was glad to hear her roommate was there. I immediately felt better that she was not at the barn alone and someone was watching her.

I started asking her questions about how she was feeling besides her heart racing. Was there any other pain or discomfort in any other parts of her body? Did she have a headache or any new sight issues? She didn't really have anything. She just said she was a little worried about how long it was lasting and wondering what to do. I suggested just sitting there for a few more minutes, trying to take some deep, calming breaths.

When the episode was not subsiding, I suggested going to the emergency room. Maybe it would remain long enough for them to finally find something. That way, we'd no longer have to wonder what was really going on. I heard her tell her roommate to get the car. I told her I loved her and we said our goodbyes.

She called me back after she was back at her dorm to tell me that, of course, the episode was over just about the time she hit the door of the hospital. She expressed how frustrating that was, but she was happy to tell me there was a diagnosis and that it wasn't as bad as I'd already dreamed up. She told me it was Orthostatic Hypotension and that the best thing she could do is not to bend over and then get back up quickly. It did require her to be more mindful when working at the farm or just moving about in general. But I was relieved it was something that just required vigilance on her part rather than drugs or surgery. We finally had a name for these crazy episodes and a way to prevent them in the future.

I said a few extra prayers for her strength and for continued healing. I also prayed a deep gratitude for her awesome roommate and friends and for keeping her with me yet again. I was a little shaken up because I felt somewhat helpless being so far away. Once again, it all worked out.

As of this writing, all seems well.

Harvest

WHAT WE WISH WE HAD

What caused the most pain for me was that I went so completely unsupported. I longed for the entire family to receive counseling to help us through this. What we needed was a systems approach. As the primary caregiver, I felt left to flounder on my own figuring out what I should or should not do or say. Yes, the eating disorder clinic provided educational materials and helped outline a nutrition plan. However, there was no additional support for anyone else in the family, all of whom were almost as equally impacted as Alexa.

The entire family needed support. Had Robert been provided with counseling, perhaps he might have gained the skills and confidence to step into the situation. I think counseling might have helped Nick understand what was going on with Alexa. Plus, he has a unique perspective on things. He might have been able to ask some questions that we couldn't answer — or at least not well — and may even have provided some insights. Most importantly, he might have had someone to talk to about how Alexa was manipulating him and provide guidance on how to manage that in a way that he didn't feel like he was going against his sister.

I had to seek out a counselor on my own. Without specific eating disorder experience, however, they couldn't provide me with the real support I needed to navigate this thing. When the two of us took a more team approach, things changed. But that was after the main services provided by the clinic. I liked the team approach because I got some counseling as an individual, Alexa got counseling as an individual and then we came together to discuss our progress and how that related to the eating disorder. If the entire family had been involved in this, it might have benefited us beyond the eating disorder and made it easier for us to talk about issues as a family, together.

In hindsight, I wish someone had suggested a weekly family meeting where we could talk about wins, tackle questions and participate in a family bonding activity of some kind.

I also wonder what might have happened if we invited other support people into counseling in some way. I think of the school counselor who might have been kept abreast of the situation and been provided specific resources for handling any issues at the school. They would have benefited from direct guidance with our situation but also continuing education for similar situations that may occur at the school. Surely, Alexa was not the first, nor the last, student at the school with an eating disorder.

I think about other eating disorder clients who either don't have immediate family or are adults living outside of the family unit. I wonder, with permission of course, how other non-immediate family members or friends willing to support people could be included in counseling in some way.

Eating disorders impact everyone close to the client. They need their own form of guidance so, at the very least, they aren't making matters worse. At best, they can be provided with tools, language, and actions that will benefit the person struggling. At a minimum, we all could have learned more about how to connect to the beautiful human underneath the disorder.

Having this approach from the start might have saved a lot of suffering — for everyone involved.

I did not know how to talk about the eating disorder with anyone around me, including Alexa. I could have used a list of things that should and should not be said to someone with an eating disorder. I had nothing that would help me explain to her what was going on, or what the plan was, or if anything would be different for someone at her young age. As such, we all made stories up in our minds instead. When that happens, it's usually not good and almost always quite some distance from the truth.

I needed a list of encouraging phrases and a reward system that could intervene when the eating disorder had taken Alexa over. It might have even been helpful to have a list of signs to watch out for when the eating disorder has been triggered. In our case, her slow eating was always there, while the strong emotional episodes were less frequent. I will never forget the empty eyes I faced during the caged animal instance. Prepared with some words of encouragement in a situation like that might have prevented us from making any urgent care visits.

I could have used some ideas for how to talk to family members outside the home and close enough to need to know what was going on. Better yet, a letter from the clinic that I could hand over, so I wouldn't have to explain it myself at all. Perhaps that list could have included a phone number for a person to contact with any questions, being clear that they wouldn't be provided with Alexa's details. It would just help them understand what was going on with Alexa and how they might also support our family.

Likewise, some guidance on who else we might consider telling and how to do that. There were only a few key people that I told. The Lee family was one of them. If Alexa was ever going over to Macy's house, they had to know what was happening. And I could only allow her to go if I knew they would provide the support we needed. The Lee family were wonderful, compassionate friends; I knew I could trust them with this information.

I felt like the school counselor needed to know to be able to support Alexa at school. I told the pastor as someone who supports our entire family, and we would all need that. He checked in with us on occasion and that was helpful.

Our family pastor and close friends might have benefited from additional knowledge and access to a person to ask questions. In our situation, I am guessing every one of the people named in our book would have happily received this information and would have likely called with questions.

As they say, it takes a village. Imagine if that village had tools and resources to assist us.

As time passed, I learned to see the eating disorder as almost a separate entity from Alexa, the person. Initially, and I hate to admit this, I was treating her as if she was the eating disorder. The eating disorder came first and the person came last. I think this was a huge mistake.

Other than "how are you today?" clinic staff, including counselors, did not ask questions that got to the person's essence and interests. Alexa has said it would have been nice if people asked her about her life on the farm or her interests at school. Heck, even just asking about her favorite color. How is she going to tell people the intimate details of what was going on with her or how she was feeling if they didn't take the time to get to know her as a person first? Some trust needs to be established for this to happen.

Yes, establishing a relationship takes time. What if they didn't even talk about the eating disorder for the first week or two of treatment to establish a relationship? Instead of me videotaping Alexa, which put me in an early position of "bad guy," the treatment team could have had a meal or two with us to get to know each other while they could also observe the eating. At that time, counselors could share a bit of personal information to begin building relationships and trust. Trust only occurs when both are solid in the relationship.

I also felt like just a number in the system, someone who provided the rides and answered a few questions here and there. I don't recall anyone asking how I was doing — at least, not to the extent they were willing to listen to my real answer.

Had some kind of relationship been built with the counselors, I might have also had more trust in how they were handling Alexa. Without a relationship, there was a distance between me and Alexa's counselors. When progress felt minimal, I had no way to approach it except to ask for another counselor — or at least that's what it felt like. Had I had a deeper relationship with our case worker, maybe I could have gone to them with my questions and concerns.

Perhaps the clinic wouldn't have felt so cold, and we might have dreaded going there less, if we had relationships with more of the people caring for Alexa. People didn't say "hi" in the hallway, they just walked past silently with eyes down. What if they set the stage by walking down the hallways warmly greeting each other more like we were friends? I wonder.

I think what I despise most about the medical model is the speed at which doctors are pushed to get people in, diagnosed, treated and out. What I love about my personal doctor is she takes the time necessary to understand what is going on with me both physically and mentally, so she can serve my whole person. When Dr. X took us to his office and told us his personal story,

I had more trust that we had someone on our side who was not just "treating" the eating disorder.

I think this relationship-building piece might also better de-stigmatize the eating disorder. All the silence and lack of human response made me feel like I should also be silent and aloof outside of the clinic. We need to make these conversations more readily available and humane.

Additionally, and from my experience, I feel the medical model would be improved by incorporating physical and emotional aspects of well-being into diagnosis and treatment. More importantly, additional resources with prevention and overall well-being as the focus would be valuable beyond treating illness after it has appeared.

Finally, below is what I wished I had posted on our refrigerator in addition to or in place of the rules. I would have taken this to appointments and asked for input as well as to discuss during weekly family meetings.

- The people Mom should reach out for support when feeling overwhelmed are _____, _____, or _____.
- Parent support group contact is _____.
- The people Alexa can reach out to for support when she feels unheard or unseen by Mom are _____, _____, or _____.
- Remember, before reacting, ask yourself "what else might be happening?"
- When feeling guilt/shame, I can do _____, _____ or _____.
- The activities that help Alexa defeat ED thoughts are _____, _____, or _____.
- The activities that help Mom rest/rejuvenate/bring joy are _____, _____, and _____.
- Responsibilities:
    - Michelle is responsible for _____, _____ and _____.
    - Robert is responsible for _____, _____, and _____.
    - Both are responsible for _____, _____, and _____.
    - Nick can help by _____, _____, or _____.

- This week's family agenda includes
  - The discussion leader is:
  - We are celebrating:
  - What went well this week is:
  - What we need to discuss this week is:
  - The schedule for next week is:
  - A fun activity we are going to do is:
- Post Loves and Joys here:

- The Bible verses to read when in overwhelm or despair are:

- The Bible verses to read to celebrate children are:

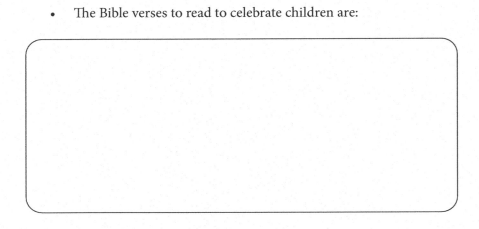

Alexa's Perspective:

Because I was so young during my eating disorder, most of the care-giving and control were left to my mom. Meal plans and nutrition in general were discussed only with mom while I sat in the waiting area. To some extent, I understand why it was that way. I likely would not have completely understood all of that information and it may have been overwhelming. Not to mention my eating disorder may have attempted to shut it out completely. However, because of this separation and lack of nutrition education for me in particular, even as I started to recover, I feel like I have no better understanding of nutrition than I did back then. I have a sense of the need to eat and the need for appropriate portion sizes, but not of how to balance the types of foods I eat and how to best fuel my body and eat in a healthy way.

I wish there would have been follow-up built into my treatment. For example, having check-ins periodically through my adolescent years would've been really helpful. As I grew older and further removed from my eating disorder, I continued to learn things about myself and about my eating. At an older age, I also would've been better equipped mentally to understand some of those nutrition principles and strategies. I started to care more about my health and have more questions about how to keep myself healthy.

In my teenage years, before going to college, I would've gained so much from having nutrition education to prepare me to make my own food choices versus my parents doing all the planning, shopping and cooking. I'm not saying this is something we couldn't have sought out ourselves, we probably should have, but for some reason it felt hard to justify seeking this type of support when I wasn't in the depths of a problem. It would've been so much easier to say yes to someone reaching out suggesting a check-in versus trying to seek it out somewhere else.

WHAT WE LEARNED

It seems impossible to say for certain all the things we learned from this journey together. To be honest, I don't know that we'll ever be done learning things from the experience. Through our writing, discussion and continued life experience, we are constantly exposing new angles, new information and new feelings. However, we'll do our best to lay out some of the highlights of what we've learned thus far.

Through this journey, we learned a lot about eating disorders. Eating disorders can look so incredibly different from person to person, and they can affect anyone. It doesn't matter your age, race, size, sex or gender identity — anyone can experience disordered eating or an eating disorder. I was only ten-years-old when I was first told I had an eating disorder. I also didn't have anorexia or bulimia, which seem to be the commonly known diagnoses; I had eating concerns that were uniquely my own. It also became apparent to us how important it was that we sought care early-on after red flags were raised. Had we waited until I had more medical concerns or more drastic symptoms, it may have been an even harder battle.

We also learned that support in our lives can be found not only in our human counterparts, but also non-human. It annoys me when people say "it's just a dog." Cisco was not and is not "just a dog" to me. Though Cisco seemingly started out as just a pet within our family, he quickly grew to become a family member, a friend and a refuge. He was nonjudgmental when I was breaking down. He was calm when I was angry. When I wanted to run, he drew near. I could talk to him about anything and he would happily sit and listen. We had our own special language with each other. His fur on my hands and pressure against my sides gave me peace. He loved me unconditionally when I didn't love myself.

I tell people to this day: Cisco saved my life.

Mom also acknowledges how much of a relief Cisco brought to her. When she was about to lose her patience with me, she knew she could send me to Cisco for the support I needed. In her words, *"there was something powerful about that one place where Alexa would be safe and accepted in whatever condition. Cisco didn't judge."*

My relationship with Cisco during my eating disorder and throughout my life has inspired me in so many ways. I completed a bachelor's degree in Anthrozoology, which is the study of human-animal interactions, alongside a bachelor's degree in psychology. During this process, I did an internship at an equine-assisted activities organization and I learned from many animal trainers with different specializations. I practiced my own skills in training animals for therapeutic purposes and analyzing research to back it up (though there is a need for more research in this area). Knowing the impact that human-animal relationships can have, I am still considering becoming a counselor and incorporating animal-assisted therapy into my work. At the very least, I will continue to be an advocate.

Along the same lines, our ability to change the venue for a while was immensely beneficial. I would recommend seeking a change of venue if you are stuck and have the ability. It does not have to be as far or vast as the Galapagos Islands — maybe just a nearby wild area. Nature has its way of helping us heal and this trip changed everything. Alexa healed, our relationship improved and I experienced a place that is part of my work today. An extra bonus was that Alexa got to experience a group of very strong women. They showed her that women can do anything they put their minds to. Unconsciously as it may have been, these women were truly a gift to all of us.

Another one of the most impactful things I learned was that there is no shame in struggling and that it's ok, even beneficial, to share your struggles. During my eating disorder, throughout middle school and most of high school, I was so ashamed of my eating disorder. I expected people to think I was weird, weak and broken beyond repair and lovability.

It's likely that most people surrounding me had no clue what I was going through. However, when I did finally open up and share, I found some of the greatest support. Sharing our struggle with Macy and her family led to support for both my mom and me, and has created an intimate, lifelong bond between us. Writing a speech around these topics in my senior year of high school led to great conversations and spread a lot of awareness. Sharing with some of my friends in college led to empathy and a community of support for each other during a huge transition in our lives. I'm hoping that writing and sharing this book will bring not only awareness, but also support for even just one person or family out there struggling.

Looking back, I also made a lot of assumptions about our church community judging our family. Part of the beauty of having a church community is you can share the not-so-great aspects of life and they can help lift you up. I didn't need to be ashamed of that day with the pancakes in church. I didn't need to be ashamed of my family's struggles because everyone has struggles. Of course, nowhere and no one is perfect, so to say there was no judgment at all is probably not true. However, I've found that more times than not, the judgment is only perceived in my head, not actual judgment at all. The people who care about us often draw closer during times of struggle, not further away. Others around us who don't know us often don't care as much as we think they do.

We've also realized through the years that recovery from an eating disorder is a continuous process, requiring time, effort and ongoing support. Achieving the goal weight marked a significant milestone, but it wasn't yet cause for major celebration. One might think something like this is a cause for a public or semi-public celebration, but it didn't happen. The doctor simply announced we had reached the goal weight. The journey had to continue as we had to navigate giving Alexa back more authority over eating decisions and achieving full recovery of both mind and body. This book is our form of celebration.

A major lesson is that eating disorders can leave lasting emotional scars on both individuals and their loved ones. As we neared completion of this book, I realized that this was a traumatic event that I had not fully processed as a parent. There is a part of my daughter's personality that was never recovered and an innocent spark between us that was nearly eliminated. In addition, the eating disorder turned me into a monster in her eyes. While I understand that sentiment, I wonder how much of this she still carries, unconsciously, of this monsterhood. A support group of parents of recovered children seems as much needed as support groups while in the midst of treatment. Understanding and processing such an overwhelming experience are crucial aspects of the healing process.

Another thing we have come to recognize through this process is just how complex the mother-daughter relationship is, especially during a time of struggle like this eating disorder journey.

On the surface, it seemed to me that Mom and I had nothing in common. She didn't understand me or listen to me, we were always fighting and I was pretty sure we hated each other. There was lots of yelling. And crying. And uncomfortable silence, just to name a few. But all of this was temporary. ED was orchestrating it all and trying to take over my mind.

Deep beneath the surface, everything that mattered still survived and would eventually come to win me back. We still loved each other so much. When my mom went away on business trips, all I wanted to do was call her or see her. Even amid the fighting and anger, and confusion, I still knew I needed my mom even if I didn't always want what she was doing. I've now come to realize that mom's actions were attempts to heal me, because she loved me. This was mom's first time learning how to battle an eating disorder just like it was my first time. We both made mistakes along the way, which is expected, but can be forgiven with time.

Alongside that, even though we were on this journey together, there were still so many things we didn't realize about each other. The biggest example of this is both of our stories about suicidal ideation. Though mom knew she was hurting me a lot by threatening to send Cisco away, she didn't realize just how much this tore me apart. She didn't know how threatening that really was to my life. I was not in a mental state to share that information, especially not with her.

Mom also struggled in her own way with suicidal ideation. This eating disorder was consuming a lot of space in our lives. With no support, she felt helpless and probably a little hopeless. When I first heard mom tell this story, I was shocked. I had no idea this had happened. It makes me sad that I was so lost in the eating disorder that I could not see mom's inner struggle at the time. I was so focused on fighting against everything that was happening to me, that I wasn't much concerned about others in the process. To think the story could've ended so differently scares me and makes me feel a little guilty. However, I have to give myself grace. I was young, struggling myself, and it wasn't my fault. Even though we were both inextricably connected in this battle, there was still so much we both didn't see.

Since both of us experience suicidal ideation, you can see how serious a diagnosis like this can feel. It is overwhelming. We urge you to find support teams early.

We also learned that through struggles like our eating disorder journey, we lost some things and we gained some things.

Before my eating disorder, I was carefree, bubbly and very unguarded with those around me. This sort of inner spark I had in my childhood now has a wall built up around it. It's not that I don't have a joyful spirit, or even that this inner spark doesn't still exist, but it somehow chipped away at my trusting and easygoing nature. A lot of things I had to encounter and learn were very mature, especially for a ten-year-old.

Meeting people who seemed to judge me without even knowing me, learning to be a master manipulator and fighting with the people closest to me made it difficult to embrace childhood life the way others might have at that age. While it's true that we all lose a little bit of childhood spark as we age, this was likely a more drastic change and came on earlier than other circumstances may have provided.

We both also lost some trust in the medical system in different ways. Medical discussions and decisions are some of the most vulnerable we encounter in our lives, and they shouldn't be made lightly.

I already had some pretty extreme medical fears due to previous experiences with needles. So, what I learned from some of the negative experiences I had during the medical visits of my eating disorder is that I really desire to have medical providers acknowledge how I feel mentally and emotionally during my visit. I want them to first respect my humanity. Being able to say "I'm honestly scared," and be heard. It would be so helpful for me if medical providers slowed down and helped me feel comfortable while processing the things that need to be done instead of asking their required questions and quickly moving through the needed procedures without acknowledging my personhood. And I need to be more confident in asking for that support.

At the eating disorder clinic, I just didn't feel like the counselors were getting to the underlying causes of Alexa's eating disorder, which caused me to lose faith in the medical system. I had to fight hard for any changes I felt were necessary. I don't have blind faith in the medical system or counseling system. I've always asked questions, but now I keep asking until I am satisfied I have all the information I need. I also work to find people who seem more suited to my needs. Medical professionals are humans, too. They can't possibly know everything, so it's okay to keep asking. It should be a learning process for everyone involved to discover and carry out the best treatment possible for each individual.

I think at that time, the recovery rate was about half or so, meaning 50% will relapse, or worse. Remember that Alexa was only ten and most of the research is based on older people. So, the information search I dove into likely led to a bleaker outlook than necessary. Perhaps I shouldn't have read that information, or at least waited until I had more information from the doctors. That is who I am, however, and it is not likely to change — even after learning from this experience.

The information available from the start is so much more extensive today. So, if you are facing this today, know that things are already better than when we started this process. Medical institutions and counselors have more information about what works and what doesn't. They are learning to be more holistic and systems-oriented in their treatment.

It is also important to note that even though the eating disorder clinic we worked with didn't ultimately feel like the best fit for us in terms of counseling and getting to the root of the struggle, they did help me to reach my goal weight and helped get us on the right track. For others, this clinic was likely just what they needed to fight their eating disorder. It's ok to say if something in your treatment is not working for you, and finding ways that do support you best. Just like every struggle is not the same, not everyone has to recover the same way.

Though it wasn't completely due to our eating disorder experience, we also lost our family unit within this journey. My parents ultimately got divorced and eventually my brother and I split time between two houses that were two hours apart. We spent weekdays and every other weekend with my mom and every other weekend with my dad. There were a lot of things we missed out on with my dad and relationships with both parents changed with time. However, I tell people often that as far as divorces go, my brother and I got it pretty good. Our parents were still friendly with each other and tried to keep big events inclusive for all of our family.

Even though the eating disorder was not what caused the ultimate breakup of our family, it was the final straw for me. I was angry at the time. Now, I realize that anger was a deep grieving — that I/we were not worth fighting for. That I did not have the skills to hold the family together, even as hard as I tried.

What I do celebrate is the way our family can be together now. It's not perfect but, over the years, I've received several acknowledgements from people about how impressed they are with how we can be around each other. Once we were separated, Robert and I both put our kids' well-being first, which meant they did not have to choose between us. I love that many of our holiday celebrations are together.

Even though we lost some things along the way, it's also so important to recognize that we also gained things as part of this journey.

Mom and I in particular gained a deeper relationship and understanding with each other than we may have had otherwise. We saw each other in very vulnerable and uncomfortable situations and we tackled some pretty unfamiliar and difficult battles. Though we maybe didn't feel the relationship strengthening in the midst of the struggle, after months and years began to go by, it was evident that we were connected in a unique and powerful way.

We learned better communication skills as part of this journey too. Unfortunately, we had to learn a lot of these skills by experiencing what didn't work but, nonetheless, we began to recognize what was helpful and what was harmful.

As Alexa started to be able to make more decisions about food, we also learned how to talk about it better. When she was struggling to eat something she normally liked, I was able to ask her what was going on. I'd ask her what she was thinking concerning the food or herself. Sometimes, it was something entirely different that was bothering her. As she got better, some of her mindset shifted to what others would think about her eating. Sometimes, we even had discussions before we went out somewhere and made agreements on how we would handle some scenarios.

When we went for holidays with my family, we would talk about the minimum she had to eat. I'd agree to let her have a few more of the things she really liked (mashed potatoes especially) and smaller portions of meat. We sort of developed some head signals for what was good enough. I made sure to protect her from anyone else trying to put food on her plate. If they managed to get it on there, I promptly removed it myself or she would hand it to me. Probably the best discussions we had was when she was going to someone else's house. After she got to her ideal weight, she had much more flexibility. But we did talk about what would happen if she didn't keep up and somehow fell back into an old pattern.

Our communication was not suddenly successful. We both had to build some trust back. She had to trust that I was making the best decisions for her at times and I had to trust that she could make good decisions on her own about food. As the trust built, we learned how to speak our minds more authentically as well as have more compassion for each other.

An honest discussion about how we were each feeling might have made this easier. Being a better person today, I would have told Alexa what was happening and that we were doing the best we could with the information available. That I would do my best to support her through it. I would have had regular check-ins with how she was feeling and thinking in a non-judgmental manner. I was not in that state of mind then.

I cannot stress enough that, as a parent, it would be beneficial to be emotionally competent and inclusive. That means welcoming any emotions as they arise, without judgment, and simply talking through them calmly.

When Alexa moved on to college and then to her own home, our communication kept shifting as our lives did. We continue to grow this relationship and our communication style as we face each new life transition. Ultimately, this more positive communication system gave us the courage to write this book.

Most importantly, we learned a lot of survival skills that continue to help us with new challenges in life. We both had to learn healthy coping skills. We gained better insight into what our natural reaction to struggle is and how to harness or overcome those reactions. We had to learn how to ask for what we needed.

One of the things I learned to do was pull myself out of rumination regarding food. I often found myself getting stuck sitting and staring at the food and getting upset about eating. When this happened, I came up with strategies to get me out of that mindset. Whether that was playing cards with my family, taking some time to pet Cisco, or listening to some music, I used new techniques to recenter myself.

When I would see Alexa slowly getting more upset about food, I learned that one of the best ways to help was to tell her to take a break and go pet her dog. When we were still using the timer, I'd pause it in those moments so she could have a break from it staring her in the face. Another strategy that sometimes worked was to get out a game or deck of cards. Our family *enjoyed those things together. Alexa could finish her food while her focus was on something else. The food was still the central character, so playing wasn't quite the same, but it was a good, temporary distraction. Sometimes, we'd just start talking about a future event coming up, like something at school or with her dog. Anything that redirected her energy to something more positive seemed to be helpful.*

Before we got much better at direct dialogue, we sometimes used notes to be able to express our feelings. Alexa would write down what she was feeling and I would respond the same. There was something about writing it down on paper that felt less confrontational. Perhaps because we had to better process it inside before we put it on paper. The writing managed to short-circuit the negativity loop we'd both get into.

Eventually, I also learned that sometimes I just needed to step away. That was quite the transition for me because I had to be so vigilant in watching her early in this disease. When I started to recognize some of the ED tactics showing up, I also realized that sometimes its job was to come after me. I became aware that the best thing I could do was walk away so I could stay grounded.

All of these gains became most evident in my senior year of high school. That year, my brother was off to college and mom and I found ourselves moving into a small apartment, just the two of us. What could have become a confined war zone instead grew into a space of comfort and laughter. We openly communicated more with each other and were able to create fun amongst a not-so-positive circumstance. We listened and better understood each other. All the things we had struggled with during our battle with the eating disorder not only got us through a challenging time together, but even helped us thrive in the process.

To this day, some of what happened just doesn't make sense. She just ate slowly and squished the food through her teeth. She didn't dress differently; exercise differently or suddenly refuse to eat a bunch of foods. Not having any trouble with food myself, or having been exposed to anyone else who did, I had no knowledge or skills prior to starting outpatient treatment through the eating disorder clinic.

The clinic was also only about a year old when we arrived, so I wonder if they, too, were still developing their methods. On top of all of that, she was only 10-years-old, which was rarer at that time. It felt like a lot of experimentation. Some experiments worked and others did not.

First and foremost, I must grant myself a lot of compassion, forgiveness, and grace. I did not know, didn't have any reason to know, how to deal with an eating disorder. It taught me about my own strength and resilience capacity (joined by lots of prayer). My kids also know that I'll do whatever it takes to support them.

I was eventually able to separate the eating disorder from the person it had taken over. That means I can't be angry at Alexa for any part of this. I'm not angry at anyone anymore, but I am sometimes still sad.

What I see in Alexa is a survivor. She has learned about her own strength and resilience capacity. She is using the lessons she learned for greater good in the world of eating disorders. In sharing our story, we hope that others learn a few things from our experience.

One of the biggest things I feel like I/we still don't completely understand and maybe never will is where this all came from. What caused this? How did it so easily invade our lives? There are so many parts of this journey we won't understand. We continue to learn more every day. All we can do is forgive ourselves, be proud of ourselves for overcoming it all and move forward to do our best every day.

There are so many things that make me feel hopeful and encouraged today in the field of eating disorder prevention and treatment. There is more research, more established best practices, and so many passionate people in this field striving to make an impact. Some of the things my mom and I felt were missing during our journey already exist in some ways today. The stigma that has historically existed surrounding eating disorders and mental health is being challenged and replaced with support, understanding, and compassion.

And we hope it's encouraging to others out there — we survived! We are thriving! There is beautiful life beyond the depths of an eating disorder!

A person's strength, resilience, courage, and love may all be tested, but they never go away, and they can win. Relationships may experience some strain, but they can adapt and be even stronger than ever. Even if you don't believe in yourself, know that there is someone out there — whom you may not even know — who believes in you.

Fruits of the Vine

HOW ARE WE NOW?

I first want to acknowledge that the specific stories I share leave Alexa's dad, Robert, in a bad light. It felt like apathy and abandonment at the time but, in the bigger picture, I know he supports the kids. Many times over the years, he went above and beyond to support all of us. I cannot thank him enough for that. Asking for my needs to be met was not demonstrated in my childhood, so it wasn't a skill I had at that time in my life. I have slowly learned to do better with that.

I have said it before, and I will say it again: I do not regret anything about our marriage except what I own as my inability to have a good relationship at that time. I did not know what a good relationship looked like and how my own childhood trauma contributed to our downfall. I own my half of the mess fully.

We have taken both kids together, as a family, to drop them off at their selected colleges. I had a ton of fun doing it and I find great joy in looking at the pictures of those events. Others also compliment us on our ability to remain a sort of family, even if it is not the "traditional" one anymore. In fact, I think one of the best conversations Robert and I ever had was on our way back from dropping Alexa off at her school in Montana. In the last hotel on the trip there was a bar attached and we were each provided one drink ticket. Nick planned to join us but had to go back to the room because they didn't let anyone under 21 inside. We really wanted our free drinks, so we stayed to enjoy them. I remember talking about our shared worries for Alexa being so far away. There was an aura of non-judgement — we were just speaking from our hearts and thoughts. We also reminisced about the times Alexa couldn't even do a sleepover and here she was, traveling across the country. I can still put myself at that bar table and, each time, I smile.

In 2022, we went together, as a family (including my mom and Alexa's boyfriend, now fiancé) to celebrate Christmas in Coeur d'Alene, Idaho. Alexa had arranged a cute cottage with four bedrooms and a nicely stocked kitchen. I put together a menu and Alexa and her boyfriend shopped for groceries and brought any extra supplies we thought we would need. I brought the supplies for our traditional Christmas craft decorations.

That year, it was a nest, representing both kids starting their own nests. We played cards (a family must), did some sightseeing and cooked Christmas dinner together over a three-day weekend. This was truly a celebration.

Later, we were all together for my nephew's wedding. Robert and Alexa stayed in the same cabin as my partner and me. We had fun. Nick was in the wedding party and they were staying in another house as a group. Alexa and I were both happy Robert was willing to take that step. It is so much fun watching our kids grow and mature and we occasionally talk about it together. Each time we do, I feel so much joy.

In 2022, we almost lost Robert to brain surgery, but he recovered relatively quickly. It reminded me that I would never want my kids to be without their dad. It also reminded me to update my will and other personal paperwork. We hope to have many more happy, healthy years.

I love listening to my kids' perspectives on things. I absolutely adore how my children help and protect each other. I am glad Alexa felt a little guilty for manipulating her brother the way she did. They have helped each other in many ways throughout their lives. In fact, I must work hard to recall times when they fought. I have learned now to shift from parent to guide as they have started their own lives. Alexa will contact me to help her make decisions and I will try to ask her questions about what she is thinking before I offer my opinion. Sometimes she gets annoyed with that because she just wants to know what I would do. It's a dance.

I absolutely adore the life she has been creating with her dogs and her partner. She sends me snaps of their cooking, gardening, and landscaping projects as well as their garage sale finds. And of course, she sends lots of pictures of her doggies. I am so happy that Cisco can spend his remaining days with her in her new home.

I am so proud of her for double majoring in Anthrozoology and Psychology. I am even more proud of the jobs she has been willing to try and how passionate she is to improve herself and her company wherever she goes. She is currently working for an organization in the eating disorder world and is considering graduate school for counseling so she can bring her experience and gifts to her work in their fullest fashion.

As for me — I still check in with a counselor occasionally. I am still digging up some of the effects of my childhood trauma and working to be more compassionate with myself. Now that we have completed this process and our story is out there, I have realized it is time for me to process some grief. There were many losses that I did not take the time to fully acknowledge. I am in a good place in my life, but I know the work will help me let go of any negative emotions that might remain.

I am taking a lens of healing to my work as well. I left the archery industry in 2016 after just about 14 years. I started my own company, which allows me more control over what I think is best. I can do what I want, when I want. I deliver leadership development and nature education that helps people connect to themselves, others and Earth.

Our experience with the Adlerian counselors led me to study this form of psychology in more depth. As a result, in 2019, I proposed a few ecopsychology workshops at a local counseling graduate school. They went so well that I eventually partnered with one of the participants in my first class who is a licensed counselor. We now offer several workshops and have created a 1-credit elective class at the school for Nature in Counseling. I bring ecology to the psychology field and take what I know about the principles of Alfred Adler to the conservation community.

All the leadership development workshops I do in the conservation community bring in some level of Adler. The most frequent one is "a misbehaving child is a discouraged child." Find the discouragement. This is true for adults as well. I do a full day on Courage & Vulnerability that brings in feelings of inferiority, an Adlerian principle. I also bring in the courage to adapt, which we all have. I have been a faculty member for the National

Conservation Leadership Institute, and I would not be doing this work if I had not learned about Adler from watching this psychology work wonders on us during the eating disorder experience.

Because much of my work challenges deeply held beliefs about work — what is allowed, what isn't, what leadership is and isn't and how trauma shows up there, I risk attack. I also know that most of the attacks are not about me at all, but about mirrors coming up to the things people do not want exposed. Having been through this experience and more, my recovery time is much shorter.

I have an amazingly supportive partner who encourages me in my work and challenges me to see things differently to improve. Because of what I have learned through navigating my own trauma, writing this book and developing a healthier relationship, I feel I am in a very blessed place.

This process has taught me that life is a continuous process of growth and it is okay to admit you could have done things better. I could have done better by including and discussing all of the emotions coming up for us. I'm sure the rules could have been better handled. I definitely regret threatening to take Cisco away. Regarding the pancake story, I would not change how I handled it. In the end, Alexa learned that I was not interested in playing a game. I meant business and she learned that. It might have been the hard way and this may be an example of how the monster label was justified. However, I truly think that if I hadn't stood firm that day, the same tactic would have been used repeatedly and she might not have survived.

I miss some of that time as a mother of young children — or more so, I enjoy reminiscing. I have also enjoyed watching my grown children take off on their own and be successful — it means I must have done something right.

Of course, writing this book together has been such an amazing journey. I have learned even more about Alexa, her experiences and how the "truth" of it all probably lies somewhere between our two stories. I have enjoyed getting to know her better and seeing her differently. I am excited for what the future has in store for us.

Some of my favorite conversations have been discussing our stories. We finally feel seen and heard. I listen more deeply to what others have to say and encourage those around me to do the same. I now cherish smaller and simpler things and I am more present to life itself.

So much amazing life has happened since my eating disorder.

High school was filled with activities and adventures, almost too many to name. I did everything from knowledge bowl to running track and many things in between. I participated in marching band all four years and became a section leader. I was captain of the bowling team for several years and advanced to conference tournaments in my final two years. I joined the speech team and gave an original oratory speech about my struggles with an eating disorder during my senior year. I graduated as one of the top students in my class.

From there, I went to college to study Anthrozoology and Psychology. I learned so much from classes, work and internship experiences. I learned how to live on my own. I gained more voice and stood up for what I believed in. I got to share passions and make connections with students, professors and colleagues. I made friends to last a lifetime. I graduated Summa Cum Laude with my double majors and a minor in Business Administration.

After a brief few months back home to help my dad recover from brain surgery, I packed up my two dogs and moved to Washington state. I am so blessed to be able to spend more time with Cisco, to have time to thank him for all he has been in my life. He now has a little dog brother, Marvel, who I adopted in my senior year of college.

I decided that eating disorder prevention and support is where my passion has been called. After graduation, I was hired by a national eating disorder treatment provider and have worked on both their admissions and outreach teams. I have met so many passionate people and learned so much from their experiences and knowledge. I have been so supported, encouraged, and uplifted by it all.

I am fortunate to be able to make trips home to see my family, and am lucky to have them fly out to visit me from time to time as well. It is a blessing to share in all life's ups and downs with the people I care about and love most.

In the fall of 2023, I got engaged to the love of my life. Together with our pups, we are continuing to learn, grow, and create a life we love. I got to ask Macy, my lifelong bestie, to be my maid of honor at our wedding. My brother will be standing by my side as a groomsman as well. I am so excited for all of the adventures to come.

And holy cow, I wrote a book!

Aspiring to write a book as a kid, I never thought this would be the book I wrote, but I am so proud. It has taken my relationship with my mom to a whole other vulnerable level. It has shown me that things you think are just crazy dreams can come true.

As we said before, there's so much beautiful life to be had through and after an eating disorder. Don't give up.

ACKNOWLEDGEMENTS

We want to express our heartfelt thanks to everyone who has impacted our lives and supported us throughout the journey of writing this book. Though we cannot name each person, your support and inspiration have been invaluable to us.

First and foremost, family and friends.

Mom, without your continuous encouragement and desire to write alongside me, this book would never be what it has become today. I am so thankful we've been able to grow together through this process. Life has thrown us some curveballs, but I've learned so much from your perseverance, adventurous spirit, and strength in being boldly you. *Alexa, you inspire me every day with your passion for work and life. You are wise beyond your years. You've helped me see this story from a broader perspective and I am honored that you've allowed me to join you here.*

Dad, you've inspired so much of the person I am today. I hope to demonstrate half of the love for others, work ethic, and positive energy you share every day. Thank you for supporting me in sharing this story. *Robert, thank you for showing our kids how relationships and support can go on despite divorce. This is a difficult story to share and I am grateful for your openness to let our story help others.*

Nick, you are the best brother a girl could ask for. You are reliable, protective, smart beyond words, and my best friend. I would not be the person I am without you. *You have been a blessing to my life in more ways than you might imagine. You have the gift of pure truth and simplification. The supportive relationship between you and Alexa gives me hope and joy every day. Plus, I love the life you are building for yourself as well. Your journey is worth a book of its own!*

Macy Lee, from the moment we met I knew you were an incredible person. I never knew how special friendship could be until you became my bestie. I'm so thankful for all the memories we have made together. You've supported me through my lowest lows and given me some of my highest highs. Lee family, thank you so much for accepting me as one of your own. You will forever be my second family. *Thank you, Macy Lee, for being the kind of friend to my daughter that I wish for every child. Your support helped Alexa not just survive but thrive. Lisa Lee, thank you for being the nonjudgmental support I needed back then. Thank you for being a great friend and providing some final advice for our manuscript. Thank you to the rest of the family just for making us feel welcome at all times.*

Chase Marquette, thank you for supporting me in finding time to write and giving me encouragement when I felt like things weren't going right. I'm excited for the many stories we will create as we promise to spend this life together.

I want to thank my friends who have supported me through all the ups and downs and encouraged me to be my authentic self. Though I can't name everyone here, Rhyana Juutilainen, Morgan Moon, Paige Dull, Arizona Duff, Kelsey Bassett, you have all played such a special part in my life and I am so thankful for each of you.

Kris Brooks, you were an angel when I felt most desperate. Thanks for your friendship, and your enduring love of bringing up children with encouragement and creativity.

I would like to thank my partner, Doug Olinger, for listening, providing additional perspective and encouraging me through the writing stage. To my long-time friends Beth Alsleben and Tammy Victorian, you heard my stories about this journey and made it okay to be an imperfect parent. To Lois Schlauderaff for crying and laughing with me and seeing me fully over those years (and more). And to my friend Amy Hatfield, who convinced me that I am a writer when I told myself otherwise.

I would also like to thank Annette Ryerson and the Zinnstarter board at Carroll College. Dr. Ryerson, while I had begun this project long before meeting you, I would not have jump-started the final stretch without your encouragement. Through Zinnstarter, I was able to fund our first round of edits and got some feedback that launched us in the right direction. For that I am so grateful.

Nicole Devereaux, your feedback during our first edit was so incredibly valuable. Your suggestions allowed us to refocus and discover a stronger path and direction for our writing. Your eye for the story helped us tell ours better.

Thanks to our two counselors from the Venn Diagram story, we were able to uncover the root of the eating disorder. Without your help, our situation might have been very different. Additionally, we've had the support of several other counselors who have guided us through this long journey. We are deeply grateful to all the amazing counselors in our lives.

Dr. Jillian Lampert and Susan Belangee, thank you so much for being some of our first readers and providing feedback from your expertise. Your work in the mental health and eating disorder fields is so impactful and we are so appreciative of your support in sharing our story.

Jona Ohm, thank you for being an outstanding editor, encourager, and accountability partner. Your keen insights, guidance, and unwavering support helped us bring this book to its completion. We deeply appreciate your dedication and commitment to shaping our work and taking it on its final journey.

And to God, all praise and glory.

ABOUT THE AUTHORS

Alexa:

Alexa grew up dreaming of writing a novel someday, but never imagined her first book would be part of her personal life journey. Her debut novel, *Grapevine: A Mother and Daughter's Tangled Journey Through an Eating Disorder* shares a raw and real glimpse into how an eating disorder can impact the individual as well as the family system. Alexa has bachelor's degrees in psychology and anthrozoology, and she currently serves as an outreach professional with a national eating disorder treatment center. Alexa is passionate about eating disorder awareness and prevention as well as sharing the power of the human-animal bond. Alexa and her fiancé live in Washington state with their two spunky pups.

Mom:

Michelle's journey as a parent has been both challenging and transformative. Navigating her son's autism spectrum disorder and her daughter's eating disorder, showcased in her debut novel, *Grapevine: A Mother and Daughter's Tangled Journey Through an Eating Disorder,* led her to explore the principles of Individual Psychology. Michelle completed the InnerMBA and holds certificates in Advanced Adlerian Psychology, Wellness Coaching, Advanced EcoTherapy, Applied Polyvagal Theory in Yoga, Trauma-informed Leadership and Executive Leadership. In addition, Michelle is a leader, coach and trainer in the conservation field, blending principles of human connection and her passion for Earth. Through her writing and teachings, she strives to leave a lasting impact, both in the conservation field and the human and non-human lives she touches.

Contact them with questions or to inquire about speaking engagements at:

https://grapevinethebook.com/
grapevinethebook@gmail.com
Instagram: @grapevinethebook
LinkedIn Michelle: https://www.linkedin.com/in/michelleldoerr/
LinkedIn Alexa: https://www.linkedin.com/in/alexa-d-6bb405139/